BRAIN BOOSTING FACTS
FOR CURIOUS MINDS
A TRIVIA BOOK FOR ADULTS & TEENS

BY

DANIEL KANE

COPYRIGHT © 2023 HHF Press
www.HHFPress.com

COPYRIGHT © 2023 HHF Press
First published 2023

All rights reserved. No part of this book may be reproduced in any form or by any electronic or mechanical means, including information storage and retrieval systems, without permission in writing from the publisher, except by reviewers, who may quote brief passages in a review.

Published in the United States of America by HHF Press
www.HHFPress.com
30 N Gould St Ste 21710
Sheridan, WY 82801

Disclaimer:

All content herein represents the author's own experiences and opinions, and do not represent medical or health advice. The responsibility for the consequences of your actions, including your use or misuse of any suggestion or procedure described in this book lies not with the authors, publisher or distributors of this book. The author or the publisher does not assume any liability for the use of or inability to use any or all of the information contained in this book, nor does the author or publisher accept responsibility for any type of loss or damage that may be experienced by the user as the result of activities occurring from the use of any information in this book. Use the information responsibly and at your own risk.
The author reserves the right to make changes he or she deems required to future versions of the publication to maintain accuracy.

TABLE OF CONTENTS

INTRODUCTION 6
EVERYTHING ON THE COVER.. 7
SURPRISING EVERYDAY USES FOR COMMON HOUSEHOLD ITEMS 9
BIZARRE WORLD RECORDS 10
DREAMS ARE NOT WHAT THEY SEEM... 11
INSULTS HAVE BEEN AROUND AS LONG AS WORDS.............................. 12
FORGOTTEN FASHION.. 14
FOOD FOR THOUGHT, OR JUST FOR EATING 15
FLEEK AF 17
DON'T READ THIS IF YOU'RE SUPERSTITIOUS 18
CELEBRITIES ARE AS WEIRD AS THE REST OF US 19
THE WORLD'S WEIRDEST FESTIVALS 20
ON THE SUBJECT OF BOOKS... 22
FAMOUS HOAXES AND PRANKS... 24
SOCIAL MEDIA RUINATION 26
EPIC FAILS 27
POLITICIANS ARE CRAZY... AND AMAZING TOO! 29
ROCK STARS DOING WHAT THEY DO BEST 30
STRANGE BUT TRUE... 31
ACCIDENTAL INVENTIONS... 33
LUCKY PEOPLE AND EVENTS 34
SLEEP IS FOR EVERYONE... 36
PERSONAL HYGIENE... 37
THE STRANGE HABITS OF ROYALTY 38
ANCIENT CIVILIZATIONS... 40
THE WORLD'S MOST UNUSUAL SPORTS 41

THE WORLD'S MOST UNUSUAL JOBS	42
CONSPIRACY THEORIES	43
STRANGE TECH HABITS	45
STRANGE FOOD CUSTOMS	46
PROCRASTINATION CAN BE USEFUL	48
CURIOUS WEDDING TRADITIONS	50
THE MOST AMAZING GHOST SIGHTINGS	51
THE EVOLUTION OF DATING AND LOVE RELATIONSHIPS	52
THINK YOU KNOW YOUR PET?	54
THE WORLD'S WEIRDEST MUSEUMS	55
PHOBIAS YOU NEED TO KNOW ABOUT	57
THE HISTORY OF THE TELEPHONE AND MODERN COMMUNICATION	58
CURIOUS FACTS ABOUT MUSIC	59
THE WORLD'S MOST UNUSUAL TRANSPORTATION METHODS	61
ALIENS AND EXTRATERRESTRIAL LIFE	62
COMIC BOOKS AND SUPERHEROES	64
THE WORLD'S MOST UNUSUAL HOLIDAYS	65
TV SITCOMS	67
HI-TECH INSPIRED BY STAR TREK	68
UNUSUAL HIGH-TECH WE TAKE FOR GRANTED	70
VIDEO GAMING	71
BOARD GAMES AIN'T BORING!	73
THE WORLD'S MOST UNUSUAL NATURAL WONDERS	75
THE WORLD'S MOST UNUSUAL NATURAL CREATURES	76
THE ART WORLD	77
UNUSUAL LAWS AROUND THE WORLD	79
DÉJÀ VU ALL OVER AGAIN...	80
CRYPTOZOOLOGY AND MYTHICAL CREATURES	81
AMAZING GARDENS	83

LET'S GO TO THE MALL HONEY... 84
THE SURREAL HUMAN SUBCONSCIOUS 86
ADVENTURES IN RADIO 87
THE STRANGEST FEDEX ALTERNATIVES 89
THE WORLD'S MOST UNUSUAL BUILDINGS 91
YOU WERE BORN TO READ THESE FACTS ABOUT PSYCHICS & ASTROLOGY 93
CAN I BORROW YOUR WHEELS ? 94
SPORTS EQUIPMENT BLUNDERS AND ADVANCEMENTS 96
AMUSEMENT PARKS YOU WISH YOU COULD VISIT 98
THE SCIENCE OF MEMORY 99
ESP 101
YOU SEE COLORS WHEN I TALK? 102
SURVIVAL MYTHS VS FACT 104
HUMANS VS. NATURE 106
EXTREME SURVIVAL STORIES 107
THE REAL COSTS OF FOOD 108
IS IT FOOD? CAN I EAT IT ANYWAYS? 110
DO MARKETERS LIE? 112
SUPERHUMAN SENSES 114
BAD-ASS WOMEN YOU SHOULD KNOW ABOUT 115
MEEEOOOWWW 119
WOOF! 121
INCREDIBLE ANIMAL ADAPTATIONS 123
MYSTERIOUS DISAPPEARANCES OF FAMOUS PEOPLE 126
THE END... OR IS IT? 129

INTRODUCTION

Hey there, you brain-hungry knowledge connoisseur! Welcome to the exhilarating roller coaster of cerebral delight that is *Brain-Boosting Facts For Curious Minds*! Buckle up, buttercup, because we're about to take you on a wild ride through the wacky, weird, and utterly wonderful world of trivia.

Whoever said learning was dull has clearly never laid eyes on this brain-buffet of tantalizing tidbits. We've scoured the earth, high and low (and maybe even a bit sideways), to bring you this rip-roaring collection of over 1500 facts that'll make your neurons do a happy dance.

Our mission is simple: we want to light up the dark recesses of your noggin with the electrifying power of knowledge, and have a total blast while doing it! From the bizarre mating rituals of your ancestors to the ridiculous inventions of yesteryear, this book has got it all. History, science, pop culture—you name it, we've crammed it into this one-of-a-kind, fun-filled tome.

Whether you're a know-it-all eager to up your game or a trivia newbie looking to spice up your intellectual life, *Brain-Boosting Facts For Curious Minds* is your one-way ticket to the land of enlightenment (with a twist of humor, of course). This ain't your grandma's encyclopedia—this is a thrill-a-minute, let's-turn-learning-on-its-head, laugh-out-loud kind of book!

So, prepare to embark on a whimsical journey that'll have you laughing, gasping, and marveling at the downright peculiarities of our world. Arm yourself with this arsenal of absurdity, and you'll never be caught without an ice-breaker, conversation starter, or pub quiz secret weapon again.

Ready to dive headfirst into this bottomless pit of brain-boosting goodness? Of course, you are! Flip the page, and let the adventure begin!

EVERYTHING ON THE COVER

- ❖ Nikola Tesla's work ethic was extraordinary, and he reportedly slept for only about two hours per night. Tesla believed that sleep was a waste of time and claimed that he never experienced fatigue. This intense dedication to his work enabled him to make groundbreaking discoveries, but also led to a rather solitary personal life. He also had a unique affinity for pigeons, and was known to have said that he loved a particular pigeon as a man loves a woman, highlighting his deep emotional connection to the birds.

- ❖ Cowboys were surprisingly skilled in the culinary arts. They weren't just experts in riding and roping; these cowhands also excelled in campfire cooking. Chuckwagon cooks, or "cookies," concocted scrumptious meals using simple ingredients like sourdough, beans, and coffee. One particularly beloved cowboy dish was the *son-of-a-gun stew*, created from the less glamorous parts of a cow, but flavorful enough to keep them coming back for more.

- ❖ Charlie Chaplin was a talented musician in addition to his acting and filmmaking skills. He was a self-taught pianist and violinist and often composed the music for his own films. Despite not being able to read sheet music, Chaplin had an exceptional ear for melodies and was able to convey his ideas to professional musicians who would transcribe and arrange the scores for him.

- ❖ While many people assume that the Earth is a perfect sphere, it's actually an oblate spheroid, slightly flattened at the poles and bulging at the equator. This irregular shape is due to the planet's rotation, which causes the equatorial region to expand outward. The difference in diameter between the equator and the poles is relatively small—only about 26 miles (42 kilometers)—but it has important implications for mapmaking and satellite navigation.

- ❖ The famous Pythagorean theorem, attributed to the ancient Greek mathematician Pythagoras, states that in a right-angled triangle, the square of the length of the hypotenuse (the side opposite the right angle) is equal to the sum of the squares of the other two sides. This theorem, often expressed as $a^2 + b^2 = c^2$, has been known and used for thousands of years, providing a fundamental principle for geometry and trigonometry.

- ❖ Saturn's iconic rings are not solid structures but rather composed of countless individual particles, ranging in size from tiny dust grains to massive chunks of ice. These particles are held in place by a delicate balance of gravitational forces from Saturn and its moons. Additionally, the rings are incredibly thin compared to their width—only about *30 feet* (10 meters) thick, while spanning up to 175,000 miles (282,000 kilometers) across.

- ❖ Astronauts aboard the International Space Station (ISS) experience a unique phenomenon known as the "Overview Effect." This term refers to the profound cognitive shift that occurs when astronauts view Earth from space, resulting in a heightened sense of interconnectedness and a deeper appreciation for the planet's beauty and fragility. Space travel also elongates the spine, causing a temporary increase of up to 3 inches in height!

- ❖ The microscopic world is home to countless single-celled organisms, known as protists, which exhibit a surprising diversity of forms and functions. Some protists, such as the bioluminescent Noctiluca, create dazzling light displays in the ocean, while others, like the predatory Didinium, use specialized structures to hunt and consume their prey. The study of these fascinating microorganisms has not only deepened our understanding of the complexity of life on Earth but also inspired new innovations in fields like biomimicry and nanotechnology.

- ❖ The common swift, known for its exceptional aerial abilities, can spend nearly its entire life in the air. These remarkable birds are capable of eating, drinking, and even sleeping while in flight. Recent studies have shown that common swifts can stay airborne for up to 10 months at a time during migration and non-breeding periods, only landing for brief periods during the breeding season.

- ❖ The hairy frog, also known as the horror frog or wolverine frog, is native to Central Africa and possesses an unusual defense mechanism. When threatened, this frog breaks the bones in its toes, which then protrude through the skin like sharp claws. The broken bones pierce the frog's skin, forming makeshift weapons that can be used to fend off predators.

- ❖ The compass was originally used for geomancy and fortune-telling, not navigation. It was likely invented in China during the Han Dynasty (206 BCE – 220 CE). These early compasses featured a lodestone, a naturally magnetized mineral, balanced on a bronze plate, pointing north-south.

- ❖ Einstein, renowned for his theoretical physics work, also co-invented the Einstein refrigerator with former student Leo Szilard in 1926. This absorption refrigerator utilized no moving parts and needed only a heat source to operate. Its efficiency and eco-friendliness were overshadowed by the rise of electric refrigerators, causing the Einstein refrigerator to never achieve commercial success. Despite his status as a genius, Einstein's early academic performance was unremarkable. He clashed with the German education system's rigidity and even had speech difficulties as a child. His rebelliousness led to expulsion by one headmaster, while another teacher predicted he would never amount to anything.

SURPRISING EVERYDAY USES FOR COMMON HOUSEHOLD ITEMS

- In case of power outages, a pencil can be used as an emergency candle. Light the graphite core and use it as a flame source.
- Dental floss can be used as a cutting tool for soft foods like cheese, cake, and brownies. To use, simply hold one end of the floss in each hand and use a sawing motion to cut through the food.
- A banana peel can be used to polish leather shoes. Rub the inside of the peel onto the leather in a circular motion, then buff with a cloth for a shiny and polished appearance.
- Use a dryer sheet to remove pet hair from furniture by rubbing it over the affected area. The static electricity from the dryer sheet will attract and remove pet hair.
- A hair dryer can help remove water rings on wood furniture caused by condensation from cold drinks. Apply heat with a hair dryer to the affected area and the ring should disappear.
- Make chocolate curls for decorating cakes or desserts with a vegetable peeler. Simply run the vegetable peeler along a block of chocolate to create delicate curls.
- Place a sponge at the bottom of a potted plant to help retain moisture and keep your plants hydrated. Soak the sponge in water before placing it at the bottom of the pot.

- Cut a potato into slices and place them on sunburned skin for relief. Potatoes contain anti-inflammatory properties that can help reduce redness and discomfort caused by sunburn.
- Wearing a rubber glove and running your hand over upholstery can create static electricity, making it easier to remove pet hair from furniture. Simply rub your hand over the affected area while wearing the glove.
- Clean your computer monitor without leaving any scratches by using the fine fibers of a coffee filter. Gently wipe the screen with the coffee filter, being careful not to apply too much pressure.
- Cat litter can be used to dehumidify a room, remove oil stains from driveways, and keep sneakers fresh. Place an open container of cat litter in a damp room to absorb moisture, sprinkle on oil stains and let sit for 10 minutes before wiping away, or place a small bag of cat litter in each sneaker to absorb odors.
- Peanut butter can be used to remove gum from hair, remove stickers from surfaces, and attract birds for birdwatching. To remove gum from hair, apply peanut butter to the affected area and gently work it out with your fingers. To remove stickers, apply peanut butter to the sticker and let it sit for a few minutes before peeling away. To attract birds, simply spread peanut butter on a bird feeder or tree trunk.

BIZARRE WORLD RECORDS

- The longest beard on a female belongs to Vivian Wheeler from the USA, measuring 17.5 inches long.
- The fastest time to pop 100 balloons by a dog is 40.59 seconds, set by a Jack Russell Terrier named Crumpet.
- The most spoons balanced on the face is held by Matthew Crawford from the UK, with 25 spoons.
- The largest gathering of people dressed as gorillas was achieved in Bristol, UK, with 1,014 people dressed in gorilla costumes.
- The longest distance cycled on a unicycle is held by Stéphanie and Raphaël Gaudry from France, who cycled a total of 1,874.5 km on a unicycle.
- The largest collection of Star Wars memorabilia belongs to Steve Sansweet from the USA, with over 300,000 items.
- The fastest time to climb up and down a staircase on hands and knees is held by Jens Stokbro from Denmark, who completed the climb in just 1 minute and 17 seconds.
- The longest distance swam underwater with one breath is held by Stig Severinsen from Denmark, who swam a total of 160 meters underwater with one breath.
- The most T-shirts put on in one minute is held by Sanath Bandara from Sri Lanka, who put on a total of 14 T-shirts in one minute.

- The longest fingernail on a single hand is held by Lee Redmond from the USA, whose right thumbnail measured 8.65 meters in length.
- The most candles extinguished by the tongue in one minute is held by Thomas Blackthorne from the UK, who extinguished a total of 33 candles in one minute.
- The longest distance skateboarded in 24 hours is held by Ammon McNeely from the USA, who skateboarded a total of 1,015.9 km in 24 hours.
- The fastest time to solve a Rubik's cube blindfolded is held by Yusheng Du from China, who solved a Rubik's cube in just 22.95 seconds.
- The most tennis balls held in the hand is held by Jyoti Amge from India, who held a total of 11 tennis balls in her hand.

DREAMS ARE NOT WHAT THEY SEEM...

- Albert Einstein is said to have come up with the theory of relativity in a dream, where he imagined himself riding on a beam of light.
- Blind people also dream, and their dreams often involve sounds, smells, and touch instead of visual images. This suggests that the content of dreams is not limited to what a person has experienced in waking life.
- Studies have shown that people tend to have more negative dreams when they sleep on their left side, and more positive dreams when they sleep on their right side. The reason for this is not fully understood, but it may have to do with the way the brain processes emotions during sleep.
- The most common recurring dream theme is being chased or pursued. This may be related to feelings of anxiety or stress in waking life.

- In a phenomenon known as "lucid dreaming," some people are able to become aware that they are dreaming and even control the content of their dreams. This can be a powerful tool for self-exploration and personal growth.
- It is estimated that about 12% of people dream only in black and white. This phenomenon may be related to the fact that black and white television was the norm until the 1960s.
- The concept of the "Sandman" who brings sleep and dreams originated in Germanic folklore. The Sandman is said to sprinkle sand or dust in the eyes of children to make them fall asleep.
- Some cultures believe that dreams are a way of communicating with the spirit world or with ancestors. In these cultures, dreams are often taken very seriously and are seen as a source of guidance and wisdom.
- Some people experience "out-of-body experiences" during dreams, where they feel like they are floating above their body or observing themselves from a distance.
- The inventor Elias Howe is said to have come up with the idea for the modern sewing machine in a dream, where he saw a group of cannibals holding spears with holes in the tips. This inspired him to invent a needle with a hole at the pointed end, which eventually led to the creation of the sewing machine.
- The poet Samuel Taylor Coleridge famously wrote the poem "Kubla Khan" after waking up from a dream where he saw a fantastical palace.
- Salvador Dali, the famous surrealist painter, was known for using his dreams as inspiration for his artwork. He claimed to have experienced vivid and bizarre dreams throughout his life.
- In a phenomenon known as "dream incorporation," people can incorporate external stimuli into their dreams. For example, a person who is sleeping with a noisy fan may dream of being on an airplane.
- The famous philosopher René Descartes believed that dreams were a way of accessing the soul and the spiritual realm, and that dreams could reveal truths that were not accessible through conscious thought.
- Some people believe that they can use lucid dreaming to overcome phobias or fears, by confronting and facing their fears in a safe and controlled dream environment.

INSULTS HAVE BEEN AROUND AS LONG AS WORDS

- The word "insult" comes from the Latin "insultare," which means "to jump on" or "to assail."

- In ancient Greece, it was common to use insults as a form of entertainment, with "insult contests" being held at public events and festivals.
- Shakespeare was known for his mastery of insults, with his plays containing over 3,000 insults and slurs.
- The phrase "lame duck" originally referred to a stockbroker who defaulted on his debts, but is now used to describe a politician or public figure who is ineffective or powerless.
- In Japan, it is considered impolite to make direct eye contact or speak too loudly, and insulting someone publicly is seen as a grave offense.
- In ancient Rome, it was common to insult someone by questioning their masculinity or virility.
- The phrase "sour grapes" comes from Aesop's fable "The Fox and the Grapes," where a fox dismisses a bunch of grapes he cannot reach as "sour."
- The word "nincompoop" is believed to have originated from the Latin phrase "non compos mentis," meaning "not of sound mind."
- In ancient Egypt, insulting someone's mother was considered one of the most serious insults, as the mother was seen as the source of life and fertility.
- The phrase "suck it up" comes from military slang and is used to tell someone to stop complaining or whining.
- The word "dunce" comes from the name of the medieval theologian John Duns Scotus, who was considered by some to be a dull and unintelligent thinker.
- The phrase "by hook or by crook" originally referred to the practice of using a "hook" or "crook" to steal wood from private land, but is now used to describe any means necessary to achieve a goal.
- The word "cretin" is derived from the French word "chrétien," meaning "Christian," and was originally used to describe people with intellectual disabilities who were cared for by Christian organizations.
- The phrase "go fly a kite" is a polite way of telling someone to go away or stop bothering you.
- The word "blatherskite" is a Scottish term used to describe someone who talks nonsense or gibberish.
- The phrase "dog's breakfast" is a British term used to describe something that is messy, disorganized, or poorly done.
- The word "dweeb" was first used in the 1980s to describe someone who is socially awkward or unpopular.

FORGOTTEN FASHION

- In the 18th century, men wore wigs that were powdered and styled to look like giant cotton candy clouds. The wigs were a symbol of wealth and status, as they were expensive to purchase and maintain.
- Before the 19th century, wearing bright colors was a privilege reserved for royalty. Textile dyeing was a complex and expensive process, and bright colors were typically reserved for the wealthy elite who could afford to commission such luxury items.
- The first documented use of a safety pin as an accessory was by punk icon Malcolm McLaren in the 1970s.
- High heels were originally designed to keep horseback riders' feet from slipping out of stirrups.
- The first high heels were actually designed for men in the 1600s, not for women as commonly believed. They were worn by upper-class men to signify their wealth and status, and the heels were often red, which further distinguished them from the common people. Women later began wearing high heels as well, but initially, it was a men's fashion trend.
- The first fashion brand to launch a clothing line made entirely out of recycled plastic was Patagonia in 1993.
- The first fashion brand to launch a collection made entirely from vegan leather was Stella McCartney (daughter of Sir Paul McCartney from the Beatles) in 2010.
- In medieval times, people believed wearing clothes inside out would ward off evil spirits.
- The first recorded use of a fashion accessory was a caveman wearing a leopard skin as a cloak.

- In ancient Greece, shoes that made noise were called kothorni or cothurni, and they were worn by actors and wealthy people to increase their stature and create a sense of grandeur when they walked.
- In medieval Europe, it was fashionable for men to wear codpieces, which were essentially pouches for their genitalia.
- In the 16th century, women wore "chopines," which were platform shoes up to 20 inches tall. These shoes were designed to protect the feet and the hem of the dress from mud and dirt on the streets, as well as to display the social status of the wearer, as only wealthy women could afford them.
- Chanel was the first designer brand to launch its own perfume in 1921, with the release of its iconic fragrance Chanel No. 5. The scent was created by the renowned perfumer Ernest Beaux, and its success paved the way for other designer brands to follow suit with their own fragrances.
- Christian Dior was the first fashion designer to launch a sunglasses collection in the 1950s, which was an instant success and helped to establish sunglasses as a fashion accessory. The sunglasses were designed to complement Dior's clothing collections and were often oversized and glamorous, reflecting the fashion trends of the time.
- The first umbrella was invented in ancient Egypt and was made from papyrus or oiled paper.
- The first pants, also known as trousers, were invented over 3,000 years ago and were worn by horseback riders in Central Asia. The pants were designed to allow for greater freedom of movement while riding and were made from materials like wool and leather.
- In Scotland, each clan had its own unique plaid pattern, which served as a symbol of identity.
- The word "polka dot" comes from the polka dance craze of the mid-19th century.
- Coco Chanel revolutionized women's fashion in the 1920s by introducing the little black dress, which was simple, elegant, and accessible to women of all social classes.

FOOD FOR THOUGHT, OR JUST FOR EATING

- The most expensive pizza in the world costs $12,000 and is topped with caviar, lobster, and gold flakes.
- The first chocolate chip cookie was invented in 1938 by Ruth Wakefield of the Toll House Inn in Massachusetts.
- In Japan, KFC is a traditional Christmas Eve dinner. This began in 1974 as a marketing campaign.
- The world's largest cup of coffee was brewed in South Korea in 2014 and measured 3,700 liters.

- The world's most expensive fruit is the Japanese Yubari melon, which can cost up to $26,000 per pair. The melons are grown in a small region of Japan and are highly prized for their sweetness, texture, and juiciness. They are often given as gifts and are considered a status symbol in Japanese culture.
- In 2018, a restaurant in Taiwan called Kao Chi created a dish called "Mosquitoes Have No Borders," which was made with 100 fried mosquitoes. The dish was meant to be a tribute to the Taiwanese night market culture, where fried insects are a popular snack.
- In Mexico, there is a type of ant called "escamoles" that is considered a delicacy and is often used in traditional dishes like guacamole and tacos.
- In Japan, they eat fugu, which is a poisonous pufferfish. Chefs must have a special license to prepare it.
- The first recorded use of hot sauce was in Ancient Rome, where they used a spicy sauce called garum on their food which was a fermented fish sauce.
- Black Ivory Coffee is made from coffee beans that are fed to elephants, and then collected from their dung after they have been naturally fermented. It is one of the most expensive coffees in the world, with a price tag of up to $500 per pound due to its rarity and labor-intensive production process.
- In some parts of Scandinavia, they eat surstromming, which is a fermented fish that has an extremely strong odor.
- In some parts of Central America, they eat iguana, which is a good source of protein and is often roasted or stewed.
- In some parts of Southeast Asia, they eat balut, which is a fertilized duck egg that has been boiled and eaten with salt and chili. Balut is a relatively inexpensive source of protein and calcium, and is considered by some to be an aphrodisiac for men.
- Tomato juice was first served as a breakfast drink in the early 1900s, and was later popularized as a mixer for cocktails such as the Bloody Mary.
- Pepsi was originally called "Brad's Drink" and was invented in 1898 by Caleb Bradham, who was a pharmacist.
- In Iceland, there is a type of liquor called "Brennivín" that is made from fermented potatoes and caraway seeds and is often referred to as "black death" due to its strong taste and high alcohol content.
- In Thailand, there is a type of fruit called "Durian" that is known for its strong odor, which has been compared to that of gym socks or rotting meat. The odor is so disturbing to people that it is illegal in certain countries to carry a Durian on public transportation.

FLEEK AF

- The phrase "the cat's pajamas" is a 1920s slang term used to describe something or someone that is stylish or fashionable.
- The term "dude" originally referred to a well-dressed man in the late 1800s, but later came to mean a guy or a friend.
- The term "busted" is slang for being caught or arrested, and comes from the idea of being caught with one's pants down.
- The term "fleek" means to be on point or stylish, and was popularized by a Vine video in 2014.
- The term "stan" means to be a fan of someone or something to an obsessive degree, and comes from the Eminem song "Stan".
- The term "finna" is a contraction of "fixing to", and means to be on the verge of doing something.
- The term "af" is an abbreviation for "as f***" and is used to intensify a statement or adjective.
- The term "shook" means to be surprised or shocked, and is often used to describe a reaction to unexpected news or events.
- The term "basic" means to be unoriginal or lacking in creativity, and is often used to describe someone who follows trends blindly.
- The term "slay" means to excel or succeed, and is often used to describe someone who is killing it or doing well.
- The term "ghosting" means to suddenly stop communicating with someone without explanation, and is often associated with online dating.
- The term "thirsty" means to be desperate or overly eager, and is often used to describe someone who is too eager for attention or validation.

- The term "clapback" means to respond to an insult or criticism in a witty or clever way.
- The term "litmus test" is a slang term used to describe a test or assessment used to determine someone's loyalty or beliefs.
- The term "spill the tea" means to gossip or share information about someone, and comes from the idea of spilling hot tea or secrets.
- "Gucci" is a slang term that means something is good or of high quality and originated in African American Vernacular English (AAVE).
- "Sus" is a shortened form of "suspicious" and is used to describe someone or something that is suspicious or untrustworthy.

DON'T READ THIS IF YOU'RE SUPERSTITIOUS

- In India, it is believed that if a person has a birthmark in the shape of a crescent moon, they have the power to control the tides.
- In Korea, it is believed that if a person dreams about a snake, they will soon receive a large sum of money.
- In India, it is believed that if you see a black butterfly, it is a sign that a loved one who has passed away is watching over you.
- In Germany, it is believed that if you drop a knife, you will have a visitor soon.
- In Greece, it is believed that if you whistle at night, you will summon evil spirits.
- In Nordic culture, it is believed that if you see a sea serpent while sailing, you should immediately turn your ship around, as it is a sign of impending danger
- In Greek culture, it is believed that if you break a mirror, you will have seven years of bad luck.
- In Hinduism, it is believed that breaking a coconut symbolizes breaking one's ego and opening oneself up to the divine.
- In ancient Egypt, it was believed that a scarab beetle symbolized the cycle of life and death, and was therefore considered a lucky talisman.
- In Russian culture, it is believed that if you whistle indoors, you will invite evil spirits into your home.
- In Great Britain, it's believed that greeting a magpie by saying "Good morning, Mr. Magpie. How is your lady wife today?" can bring good luck, while seeing a lone magpie is considered a sign of bad luck. Adding "One for sorrow, two for joy!" to the greeting is said to prevent the magpie from stealing shiny objects.
- In Germany, it's considered unlucky to congratulate someone before their actual birthday due to a superstition that demons might hear the good wishes. When toasting with Germans, it's customary to look everyone in the eyes to avoid accidentally drinking poison and to prevent any negative impact on your love life.

- In Poland, it's believed that leaving bags on the ground can make money jump out of them, so it's best to keep them off the floor.
- In Italy, Friday the 17th is considered an unlucky day, and people avoid doing anything, especially celebrating special events or wearing purple. If you find yourself in a difficult situation, there are ways to combat the bad luck, such as touching your left breast with your right hand if you're a woman, but it might be best to avoid the risk of embarrassment.
- In Vietnam, skincare is taken seriously as sleeping with makeup on is believed to attract demons.
- In Japan, the number 4 is associated with "death" and the number 9 with "suffering" due to their similar pronunciations. As a result, gifts and apartment buildings often avoid including these numbers, such as skipping the fourth floor and apartment numbers with the number 4, to prevent bad luck.
- In some parts of Europe, it is believed that opening an umbrella indoors can bring bad luck because it is said to summon evil spirits.
- In some parts of Asia, it is believed that eating a twin banana can bring bad luck and misfortune because it symbolizes separation or division.
- In some parts of Africa, it is believed that if a pregnant woman looks at a lunar eclipse, her child will be born with a cleft lip or other deformity.

CELEBRITIES ARE AS WEIRD AS THE REST OF US

- Before becoming an actor, Brad Pitt supported himself by dressing up as a chicken for the restaurant chain, El Pollo Loco.
- Lady Gaga's real name is Stefani Joanne Angelina Germanotta.

- John Lennon's last autograph was on a copy of his album "Double Fantasy," which he signed for his killer, Mark David Chapman, just hours before he was shot.
- Samuel L. Jackson has a clause in all of his movie contracts that allows him to play golf during filming.
- Jim Carrey used to be homeless and lived in a VW bus.
- Angelina Jolie has a tattoo of the coordinates of the birthplaces of all six of her children.
- Marlon Brando refused to memorize his lines for the movie "The Godfather" and instead had them written on cue cards and placed around the set.
- Demi Moore's mother tried to sell her for $500 when she was a child.
- Nicolas Cage once spent $150,000 on a pet octopus.
- Oprah Winfrey's name was supposed to be Orpah, after a character in the Bible's Book of Ruth. But since her family was unfamiliar with the name, they pronounced and spelled it "Oprah" since birth.
- Emma Stone's first acting job was a TV commercial for a dog shampoo.
- Hugh Jackman used to work as a clown for children's birthday parties.
- Neil Patrick Harris is a professional magician and has performed at the Magic Castle in Hollywood.
- Natalie Portman is fluent in Hebrew and has a degree in psychology from Harvard University.
- Matthew Perry, who played Chandler Bing on the hit TV show "Friends," once beat up Canadian Prime Minister Justin Trudeau in elementary school.
- Julia Roberts once left her husband, Lyle Lovett, to go on a date with Denzel Washington.
- Dwayne "The Rock" Johnson's father was a professional wrestler, and his maternal grandfather was a professional wrestler and promoter.
- Mandy Moore, who is best known for her acting and singing careers, climbed to the base camp of Mount Everest in 2019.
- The musician Prince was a Jehovah's Witness and would go door-to-door to talk about his faith.

THE WORLD'S WEIRDEST FESTIVALS

- La Tomatina Festival, Spain: This festival, held in Buñol, Spain, involves tens of thousands of people throwing overripe tomatoes at each other in the streets.
- Boryeong Mud Festival, South Korea: Held annually in Boryeong, this festival features mud wrestling, mud slides, and other mud-based activities.

- Kanamara Matsuri, Japan: Also known as the "Festival of the Steel Phallus," this festival is held in Kawasaki and celebrates, well, the phallus. It is said to bring good luck and fertility.
- Up Helly Aa Festival, Scotland: This festival involves a procession of men dressed as Vikings who march through the streets carrying torches. It is a celebration of the heritage and traditions of the Vikings.
- The El Colacho Baby Jumping Festival, Spain: This festival involves men dressed as devils jumping over babies lying on mattresses in the street. It is believed to ward off evil spirits and protect the babies from harm.
- Monkey Buffet Festival, Thailand: Held annually in Lopburi, Thailand, this festival involves setting out a massive feast for the local monkeys, who are free to roam and eat as they please.
- Cheese Rolling Festival, England: This festival, held in Gloucester, involves rolling a wheel of cheese down a steep hill and chasing after it. The first person to reach the bottom and grab the cheese wins.
- Hadaka Matsuri, Japan: Also known as the "Naked Festival," this festival involves thousands of men in loincloths running through the streets in a competition. Participants believe that taking part in the festival will cleanse them of their sins and bring them good luck.
- The Mohácsi Busójárás is a traditional winter festival held in Mohács, Hungary, where participants dress in elaborate masks and costumes march through the streets to scare away winter and bring in spring. The festival features music, dance, and food, and is a celebration of community, history, and the arrival of spring.
- The North Carolina Merfest Mermaid and Merman Festival is an annual event held in North Carolina, USA, that celebrates the mermaid and merman lifestyle and culture. Participants dress up as mermaids and mermen and participate in a variety of activities, such as swimming, dancing, and games, to showcase their love for the mythical creatures.
- Els Enfarinats Festival, also known as the Flour Fight Festival, is an annual event held in the Spanish town of Ibi, Valencia. It involves a massive food fight in which participants throw flour, eggs, and firecrackers at each other in the streets to celebrate the end of winter and the arrival of spring.
- The Kukeri Festival is a traditional festival held in Bulgaria, where participants dress up in elaborate costumes made of animal skins and masks with large bells attached. The festival is meant to scare away evil spirits and bring good luck for the coming year, and participants parade through the streets, making noise and dancing to traditional music.
- The Battle of the Oranges Festival is an annual event held in the Italian city of Ivrea, where participants throw oranges at each other in the streets to commemorate a medieval battle. The festival is a celebration of the triumph of good over evil and a way for people to have fun and let off steam.

- ❖ The Night of Krampus is a traditional festival held in parts of Europe, particularly in Germany and Austria, where participants dress up as the mythical creature Krampus and roam the streets making noise and scaring children. The festival is meant to be a counterpoint to the more cheerful Christmas celebrations, and is intended to serve as a reminder of the consequences of misbehavior.
- ❖ The Pot Throwing Ceremony is an annual event held in Corfu, Greece, where participants throw pots, pans, and other kitchen items out of their windows to celebrate the end of the old year and the arrival of the new. The festival is a way for people to rid themselves of bad luck and start the new year fresh, and is marked by loud noise, cheering, and feasting.
- ❖ The Hot Tub Movie Club Festival is an event where participants gather to watch movies in hot tubs. The festival is a unique way to combine the relaxing experience of soaking in a hot tub with the enjoyment of watching films, and often features a lineup of classic and cult films.
- ❖ The Bridport Hat Festival is an annual event held in Bridport, England, where participants showcase and compete with their creatively designed hats. The festival is a celebration of millinery arts and a way for hat enthusiasts to come together and showcase their skills and designs.
- ❖ The Puli Kali festival is an annual event held in the Indian state of Kerala, where participants paint themselves and dress up in elaborate tiger costumes. The festival is a celebration of the harvest season and is marked by street performances, music, and dance, and is considered an important part of Kerala's cultural heritage.
- ❖ Thaipusam is an annual Hindu festival held in Malaysia, where participants carry large metal kavadis (structures) attached to their bodies as acts of devotion to the deity Lord Murugan. The festival is marked by colorful processions, music, and dance, and is considered a time for spiritual renewal and purification.
- ❖ The Toe Wrestling Championship in England is a competition where participants go toe-to-toe (or foot-to-foot) in a test of strength and endurance.

ON THE SUBJECT OF BOOKS...

- ❖ The most translated book in the world after the Bible is the children's storybook "The Little Prince" by Antoine de Saint-Exupéry.
- ❖ The shortest novel ever written is "Brief Interviews with Hideous Men" by David Foster Wallace, which consists of only twenty-six pages.
- ❖ "The Catcher in the Rye" by J.D. Salinger was originally intended for adult readers but is now often taught in high schools.
- ❖ The first ever printed book was the Gutenberg Bible, produced in 1455.
- ❖ The first book ever printed in English was "The Recuyell of the Historyes of Troye," a translation of a French book, printed in 1475.

- The largest library in the world is the Library of Congress in Washington D.C., which holds over 158 million items.
- The word "nerd" was first coined by Dr. Seuss in his book "If I Ran the Zoo."
- The first book ever written on a typewriter was Mark Twain's "The Adventures of Tom Sawyer."
- The most expensive book ever sold was Leonardo da Vinci's Codex Leicester, which sold for $30.8 million in 1994.
- The fastest selling book of all time was J.K. Rowling's "Harry Potter and the Deathly Hallows," with 8.3 million copies sold in its first 24 hours.
- The first book ever banned by the U.S. government was Thomas Paine's "Rights of Man," which was banned in 1792 for advocating revolutionary ideas.
- The most stolen book in the world is "The Adventures of Huckleberry Finn" by Mark Twain.
- The book "To Kill a Mockingbird" by Harper Lee was originally rejected by publishers because it was deemed "not really a novel."
- The longest novel ever written is "A la recherche du temps perdu" by Marcel Proust, which consists of over 1.5 million words.
- The first book ever written in English by a woman was "Reveille: The Dawning of the Reformation in England" by Margaret Tyndal, published in 1534.
- The most expensive book ever printed was the Gutenberg Bible, which cost over $3 million to produce in today's dollars.
- The first book ever written in the United States was "A Day in the Life of Ebenezer Mattock" by Samuel Danforth, published in 1678.
- The first book ever written on a computer was "A Brief Introduction to the Basic Operating System" by Frederick P. Brooks, published in 1965.
- The first book ever printed in color was "The Missal of Saint Gertrude," printed in 1497. The book was printed using a technique called xylography, or woodblock printing, which was a common printing method at the time. Each color in the book required a separate woodblock, which made the printing process time-consuming and expensive.
- The longest sentence ever published in a book is 823 words long and can be found in "Les Misérables" by Victor Hugo. The sentence is in the novel's second volume, titled "Cosette."
- The book "The Wonderful Wizard of Oz" by L. Frank Baum was originally published in 1900 with a different title: "The Wonderful Wizard of Oz: A Fairy Tale for Children." It was later shortened to just "The Wonderful Wizard of Oz."
- In the 16th century, it was common practice to "marry" books. Bookbinding was an expensive process, so people would often bind together several small books into one larger one to save money. The process was called "marrying" the books.

FAMOUS HOAXES AND PRANKS

- ❖ The Trojan Horse, one of the most famous pranks in history, was a wooden statue of a horse that the Greeks used to trick their way into the city of Troy during the Trojan War.
- ❖ In 1957, the BBC aired a hoax documentary about spaghetti trees, which claimed that spaghetti grew on trees. Many viewers were fooled and called the BBC to ask how they could grow their own spaghetti trees.
- ❖ The alien autopsy hoax of 1995 involved a fake film purporting to show the autopsy of an extraterrestrial being that was allegedly recovered from the Roswell UFO crash site in 1947.
- ❖ The Cardiff Giant, a 10-foot tall stone statue that was "discovered" in 1869 in Cardiff, New York, was revealed to be a hoax created by a man named George Hull.
- ❖ In 2009, a group of artists in London staged a fake moon landing on the roof of a building, complete with a replica of the Apollo 11 lunar module and "astronauts" in spacesuits.
- ❖ In 1938, a radio broadcast of War of the Worlds by Orson Welles caused widespread panic, as listeners believed that the simulated news reports of an actual Martian invasion were real.
- ❖ The "Balloon Boy" hoax of 2009 involved a family in Colorado who claimed that their 6-year-old son had floated away in a homemade helium balloon, only for the boy to be found hiding in the attic of their home.
- ❖ In the 19th century, P.T. Barnum was famous for his hoaxes and stunts, including the "Feejee Mermaid," a fake mermaid made from the torso of a monkey and the tail of a fish.

- In 2008, a group of artists in San Francisco staged a fake zombie invasion, complete with actors dressed as zombies roaming the streets.
- In the 1990s, a man named Alan Abel created a number of hoaxes, including the Society for Indecency to Naked Animals, which claimed to cover up naked animals to protect their modesty.
- The "Crop Circle" mystery of the late 20th century involved a series of elaborate patterns that appeared in crops fields, which were later revealed to be the work of hoaxers.
- In 1997, a group of artists in Australia staged a fake political rally, complete with actors posing as political leaders and a fake news crew reporting on the event.
- The "Hollow Earth" theory, which posits that the Earth is hollow and contains a central sun, has been discredited but continues to be the subject of hoaxes and pranks.
- In the 1970s, a man named "Kilroy" became famous for his prank of leaving his signature, "Kilroy was here," in public places all over the world.
- In the 18th century, a man named Giovanni Battista Becherini became famous for his prank of pretending to have a pet dragon that he would "ride" through the streets.
- In the 20th century, a man named Josef Dougherty became famous for his prank of pretending to be a time traveler from the year 2070, complete with futuristic clothing and gadgets.
- In the 19th century, a man named George C. Parker became famous for his series of land scams, in which he sold people fake deeds to famous landmarks, including the Brooklyn Bridge.
- The "Jackalope" is a legendary creature that is said to be a jackrabbit with antlers, but it is widely considered to be a hoax.
- In 2006, a group of artists created a fake street sign in New York City that read "Baldwin Ave" in honor of actor Alec Baldwin. The sign remained up for several hours before it was removed by authorities, and the prank was widely reported in the media.
- In the 19th century, people would tie a horse to a post and cover it with a blanket, pretending it had vanished. This prank was called "horse phantoming."
- In the 1950s, people would call their friends and ask them to turn on their porch light, saying that a telegram messenger was on the way with an urgent message. Once the porch light was turned on, the prankster would throw flour or feathers on the porch to make a mess.
- In the 1970s, people would put clear tape over the optical sensor of someone's computer mouse, rendering it useless.

SOCIAL MEDIA RUINATION

- The first social media website, Six Degrees, was launched in 1997 and allowed users to create profiles and make friends with other users.
- Facebook was originally called "Thefacebook" and was launched in 2004 exclusively for Harvard University students.
- The "like" button on Facebook was originally intended to be called the "awesome" button.
- Twitter was originally called "twttr" and only allowed 140 characters per tweet.
- The first YouTube video, uploaded in 2005, was titled "Me at the zoo" and featured co-founder Jawed Karim.
- The most-followed person on Instagram is currently Portuguese soccer player Cristiano Ronaldo with over 270 million followers.
- Social media addiction is a recognized disorder and can lead to symptoms similar to drug addiction.
- The hashtag symbol (#) on social media was originally known as the pound sign.
- The first social media platform to introduce the concept of live streaming was Justin.tv in 2007.
- LinkedIn is the oldest social media platform still in operation, having been founded in 2002.
- The most popular social media platform in Japan is Line, which has over 187 million users.
- The first YouTube video to reach 1 billion views was Gangnam Style by PSY.
- The most popular social media platform in Russia is VKontakte, which has over 97 million monthly users.
- The most popular social media platform in China is WeChat, which has over 1 billion monthly users.
- The most popular social media platform for people over the age of 65 in the United States is currently Facebook.
- The most popular social media platform in India is currently WhatsApp, with over 400 million users.

EPIC FAILS

- In 2013, a man in the UK tried to rob a convenience store using a banana as a weapon. The man threatened the store clerk with the banana, but fled the scene empty-handed when the clerk refused to hand over any money.
- The Titanic was originally designed with 64 lifeboats, but in an effort to make it look more aesthetically pleasing, the number was reduced to 20, resulting in the loss of many lives during its sinking.
- The Chernobyl disaster, a nuclear accident that occurred in 1986, was caused by human error and poor design of the reactor, resulting in the release of radioactive material and the death of many people.
- The failure of New Coke, a reformulation of Coca-Cola in 1985, was a result of public backlash against the change and a strong emotional attachment to the original formula.
- The Mars Climate Orbiter, a space probe sent to study Mars in 1999, was destroyed on arrival due to a miscalculation of the units used in its software.
- The Great Wall of China, an engineering marvel, ended up being a glorified tourist attraction that did little to protect China from invasions.
- In 2018, the "Tide Pod Challenge" went viral on social media, with people filming themselves eating laundry detergent pods, leading to health concerns and warnings from authorities.
- In 2009, an Australian man tried to sell New Zealand on eBay, but the auction was quickly taken down due to its violation of eBay's policies.
- In 2006, the Icelandic government ran an ad campaign to attract tourists to the country, but one of the slogans, "Pure. Unspoiled. And very, very cold," was widely criticized for being uninviting and off-putting.

- In 2013, a British man changed his name to "Bacon Double Cheeseburger" in honor of his favorite fast food item.
- In 1996, a French company called "Souleance" tried to sell bottled oxygen to people as a health supplement, but the company went bankrupt after only a few years.
- In 2019, a man in the US tried to rob a bank but accidentally gave the teller his own ID, leading to his arrest.
- In 2014, Burger King tried to market a low-calorie "Satisfries" option, but they failed to catch on and were eventually discontinued.
- In 1997, "Batman and Robin," starring George Clooney and Arnold Schwarzenegger, was widely criticized for its campy tone and over-the-top performances, and is often cited as one of the worst superhero movies ever made.
- In 2020, a gender reveal party in California started a wildfire that burned over 22,000 acres and forced hundreds of people to evacuate their homes.
- In 1957, the Soviet Union sent a dog named Laika into space, but she died a few hours later due to overheating.
- The 2007 Boston Mooninite panic, where a guerrilla marketing campaign for the TV show "Aqua Teen Hunger Force" led to the city of Boston declaring a state of emergency after mistaking the LED light-up devices for bombs.
- In 1997, a group of thieves stole the entire town of Bridgeville, California, including the post office, fire station, and a number of homes. They tried to sell the town to a buyer in Arizona, but the deal fell through when they couldn't produce the title deeds.
- In 2009, a man in South Africa tried to rob a bank using a toy gun, but was foiled when the teller pointed out that the gun was fake. The man fled the scene, but was later arrested when police found him hiding in a nearby tree.
- In 2013, a man in the UK tried to break into a prison using a cucumber as a weapon. The man was quickly arrested by police, who were amazed by his choice of weapon.
- In 2018, a farmer in Germany tried to move a beehive by tying it to the back of his car and driving down the road. The beehive broke apart during the journey, causing a swarm of angry bees to attack the farmer and his car.
- In 2019, a man in the US tried to capture a squirrel by putting peanut butter on his head and lying down on the ground. The man was covered in peanut butter and surrounded by squirrels, but was unable to catch the squirrel he was trying to catch.

POLITICIANS ARE CRAZY... AND AMAZING TOO!

- Julius Caesar was kidnapped by pirates when he was 25, and demanded they raise his ransom, and even joked with them that he would come back to capture them.
- Benjamin Franklin was the oldest person to sign the US Constitution at age 81.
- Former US President George W. Bush has an asteroid named after him called "4335 George W. Bush."
- In 1960, the US presidential debate between Richard Nixon and John F. Kennedy was the first to be televised.
- Vladimir Putin was a KGB spy before he became the President of Russia.
- Kim Jong-un, the current leader of North Korea, was educated in Switzerland under a pseudonym.
- Nelson Mandela was the first black president of South Africa, and spent 27 years in prison before being released.
- Winston Churchill was a prolific writer, and won the Nobel Prize in Literature in 1953.
- Ronald Reagan was a Hollywood actor before he became the President of the United States.
- Angela Merkel, the former Chancellor of Germany, has a PhD in physics.
- Barack Obama won a Grammy Award in 2006 for the audio version of his book "Dreams from My Father."
- Queen Elizabeth II of the United Kingdom has met with more than 12 US Presidents during her reign.
- John F. Kennedy Jr. was a qualified pilot and had his own private plane.
- Abraham Lincoln is the only US president to hold a patent, for a device to lift boats over shoals.
- Mahatma Gandhi, the leader of the Indian independence movement, was nominated for the Nobel Peace Prize five times but never won.
- Joseph Stalin, former leader of the Soviet Union, was a seminary student before becoming involved in politics.
- Al Gore, former US Vice President, was the inspiration for the character of "ManBearPig" on the TV show South Park.
- Teddy Roosevelt, former US President, once gave a speech with a bullet lodged in his chest.
- John Quincy Adams, former US President, regularly swam in the Potomac River, sometimes naked.
- Thomas Jefferson, former US President, spoke six languages, including Latin and Greek.

ROCK STARS DOING WHAT THEY DO BEST

- David Bowie, known for his androgynous stage presence and innovative music, once lived in a Berlin apartment with Iggy Pop and the two of them were known for their wild and drug-fueled parties.
- Paul McCartney's first instrument was a trumpet.
- Elvis Presley was a natural blond, but he started dying his hair black when he became famous.
- Jimi Hendrix was a trained paratrooper who was honorably discharged from the U.S. Army.
- The Beatles were originally called The Quarrymen.
- Kurt Cobain was once expelled from high school for vandalizing the school property.
- Ozzy Osbourne, lead singer of Black Sabbath, once bit the head off a live bat on stage, mistaking it for a toy.
- Jim Morrison was a published poet and wrote several books of poetry.
- The Rolling Stones' song "(I Can't Get No) Satisfaction" was written in a hotel room in Clearwater, Florida.
- AC/DC's song "Highway to Hell" was written as a tribute to singer Bon Scott, who died from alcohol poisoning.
- Mick Jagger was a student at the London School of Economics before he dropped out to pursue music.
- Pink Floyd's song "Wish You Were Here" was written about their former band member Syd Barrett, who left the band due to mental health issues.
- Eric Clapton was inducted into the Rock and Roll Hall of Fame three times, once as a solo artist and twice as a member of different bands.

- Metallica's song "Enter Sandman" was inspired by the nightmares lead singer James Hetfield experienced as a child.
- The Beatles' song "Hey Jude" was originally titled "Hey Jules" and written for John Lennon's son Julian.
- Eddie Van Halen was once invited to join Kiss, but turned down the offer.
- The Doors' song "Light My Fire" was originally over seven minutes long, but was shortened for radio play.
- Jimi Hendrix was the opening act for The Monkees in 1967, but was dropped from the tour after just a few shows due to complaints from their fans.
- Prince was a huge fan of the TV show "The Simpsons" and even made a guest appearance on an episode in 2006.
- The Beatles' song "Lucy in the Sky with Diamonds" was rumored to be about the drug LSD, but John Lennon claimed it was inspired by a drawing his son Julian made of his classmate Lucy.
- Johnny Cash, known as the "Man in Black," once staged a concert inside a maximum security prison, performing for the inmates.
- Keith Richards, guitarist of The Rolling Stones, has been known to snort his father's ashes mixed with cocaine.

STRANGE BUT TRUE...

- The shortest war in history was between Britain and Zanzibar, which lasted only 38 minutes. The conflict arose when the pro-British Sultan of Zanzibar died and a rival seized power, leading to a British bombardment of the palace and the installation of a new, pro-British Sultan.
- It is physically impossible for pigs to look up at the sky. Pigs have a unique skeletal structure that makes it difficult for them to tilt their heads up and look directly at the sky.
- The world's oldest piece of chewing gum is over 9,000 years old.
- In Japan, there is a train station that has no entrance or exit. It was built for a shrine that is located nearby and has no purpose other than to allow passengers to admire the scenery.
- The entire internet weighs about the same as a single large strawberry.
- The world's deepest postbox is located in Susami Bay, Japan and is situated 10 meters underwater. This unique postbox allows visitors to send letters and postcards from the depths of the ocean, providing a truly one-of-a-kind experience. To use the postbox, visitors must take a dive into the bay and swim down to the 10-meter depth where the postbox is located.
- The longest time between two twins being born is 87 days. This is a rare and unusual occurrence, as most twins are born within minutes or hours of each

other. In this case, the first twin was born naturally and the second twin was born via a planned cesarean section 87 days later.
- There is a species of jellyfish that is immortal and can potentially live forever.
- If you shuffle a deck of cards properly, the resulting order has likely never existed before in the history of the universe.
- The longest wedding veil was longer than 63 football fields.
- The shortest commercial flight in the world lasts only 90 seconds.
- A small child could swim through the veins of a blue whale.
- The first recorded use of the word "OMG" was in a letter to Winston Churchill in 1917.
- A cockroach can live for several weeks without its head.
- The largest living organism on Earth is a fungus that covers 2,200 acres in Oregon.
- The shortest poem in the English language is "I am" by John Clare, a 19th-century English poet. The poem consists of only two words and is considered one of the simplest and most direct poems in the English language. Despite its brevity, the poem is powerful and evocative, with its two words serving as a statement of existence and individuality.
- The oldest word in the English language is "town".
- In the 1970s, a Welsh farmer successfully sued the government after a UFO allegedly landed on his property and damaged his fields.
- Humans are not the only animals that can get a suntan - some species of frogs can also get darker skin from exposure to sunlight.
- The world's largest snowflake on record measured 15 inches wide and 8 inches thick, and fell in Montana in 1887.
- The world's largest ball of twine was made by a single person, Francis A. Johnson, over a period of 29 years. The ball weighs over 17,000 pounds and is over 12 feet in diameter.
- In 1979, a Vela satellite detected a double flash of light over the Indian Ocean, which was believed to be a nuclear explosion. To this day, it is still unclear what caused the flash, as no evidence of a nuclear explosion was found.
- The world's largest potato chip was made by the Pringle's company in 1991. The chip measured 23 inches by 14 inches and weighed over 5 ounces.
- There is a hotel in Sweden that is entirely made of ice, called the Icehotel. Each winter, the hotel is rebuilt using snow and ice from the nearby Torne River, and features ice sculptures and artwork throughout.
- In the early 20th century, a popular form of entertainment was "book bowling," a game where players would stack books into a pyramid shape and then roll a bowling ball at them to knock them down. The game was especially popular in libraries and bookstores.

ACCIDENTAL INVENTIONS

- The Frisbee was invented by accident when a group of college students in Connecticut started throwing around a pie tin from the nearby Frisbie Baking Company.
- The Slinky was invented by accident when an engineer dropped a spring and saw it bounce down a flight of stairs.
- Chocolate chip cookies were invented by accident when Ruth Wakefield, the owner of the Toll House Inn, ran out of baker's chocolate and substituted it with broken pieces of Nestle chocolate bars.
- The microwave oven was invented accidentally when an engineer working on radar technology noticed that the candy bar in his pocket had melted while standing near the radar magnetron.
- Silly Putty was invented by accident when an engineer was trying to create a substitute for rubber.
- Post-it notes were invented by accident when a scientist at 3M was trying to create a strong adhesive.
- Play-Doh was invented by accident when a wallpaper cleaner was repurposed into a children's toy.
- The first artificial sweetener, saccharin, was discovered accidentally by a chemist who forgot to wash his hands after a day at the lab and tasted the sweetness in his food that evening.
- The first antibiotic, penicillin, was discovered by accident when Alexander Fleming noticed that a mold called Penicillium notatum had contaminated a petri dish.
- The Popsicle was invented by accident when an 11-year-old boy left a cup of soda with a stir stick outside in freezing temperatures.

- The potato chip was invented by accident when a chef at a restaurant in Saratoga Springs, New York, sliced a potato too thin and fried it.
- The first synthetic dye, mauveine, was discovered accidentally by a chemist who was trying to create a cure for malaria.
- The slotted spoon was invented by accident when a man trying to stir a pot of soup with a fork accidentally bent the tines and realized it could be used to strain solids.
- Safety glass was invented by accident when a French chemist discovered that a broken flask of nitrocellulose had not shattered, but instead had stayed intact.
- Viagra was invented by accident when scientists were testing a new drug for heart disease and noticed a certain side effect.
- The smoke detector was invented by accident when a scientist was trying to develop a sensor to detect poisonous gas.
- The inkjet printer was invented by accident when a Canon engineer accidentally touched a hot soldering iron to a syringe full of ink and noticed it squirted out in droplets.
- The ice cream cone was invented by accident when a vendor at the World's Fair in St. Louis ran out of bowls and started using waffles instead.
- The heart pacemaker was invented by accident when an electrical engineer named John Hopps discovered that a high-frequency oscillator he was working on could stimulate the heart.
- Stainless steel was invented by accident when Harry Brearley, a metallurgist, was trying to find a better material for gun barrels and noticed that a particular alloy he had made did not rust.
- The Slingshot - The slingshot was created by a hunter who accidentally dropped his bow and arrow and noticed that the arrow could be launched using the flexible branch that had fallen from the tree. He then developed a Y-shaped tool with a pocket in the center to hold the projectile, and the slingshot was born.
- The Safety Pin - Walter Hunt, an inventor, was trying to pay off a debt in 1849 when he came up with the idea for the safety pin. He created a simple wire with a clasp at one end that could be used to fasten clothing, and the safety pin was born.

LUCKY PEOPLE AND EVENTS

- The odds of getting struck by lightning in your lifetime are around 1 in 15,000, but the odds of winning the lottery are much lower. Roy Sullivan got struck by a lightning 7 times, and is a park ranger in the United States who holds the Guinness World Record for the most lightning strikes survived. But he still hasn't won a lottery.
- The odds of being born on a leap day are 1 in 1,461.

- The highest number of children born to one woman is believed to be 69, by a woman named Valentina Vassilyeva in the 18th century.
- The odds of being attacked by a shark are around 1 in 11.5 million.
- A man named Frane Selak has survived a plane crash, train derailment, bus crash, and car crash, and then went on to win the lottery.
- The oldest recorded person to ever live was Jeanne Calment, who lived to be 122 years and 164 days old.
- The luckiest building in New York City is believed to be the Flatiron Building, which has been the site of many miraculous escapes and other lucky events. Some people believe that the unique shape of the building creates a powerful vortex of positive energy, which attracts good luck and protects those who are inside.
- In 1975, a woman named Vesna Vulović survived a 33,000-foot fall from an airplane after a bomb exploded on board.
- In 2017, a man named Curtis Holt survived being struck by lightning twice in the same day.
- In 2007, a man named Kevin O'Connor survived a 6-foot-long piece of steel rebar impaling his skull in a construction accident.
- In 1945, a Japanese man named Tsutomu Yamaguchi survived both the atomic bombings of Hiroshima and Nagasaki, making him the only known survivor of both events.
- In 2016, a man named Dylan McWilliams survived a bear attack, a rattlesnake bite, and a shark attack, all within a three-year period.
- In 2011, a man named Chuck Raymer survived being hit by a train while attempting to take a photograph on a railroad track.
- In 2010, a man named Ed Houben became the world's most prolific sperm donor, fathering over 100 children through natural insemination.
- In 2010, a man named Harrison Odjegba Okene survived being trapped in a capsized ship at the bottom of the ocean for three days before being rescued.
- The iconic Hollywood sign was originally built as a temporary advertisement for a real estate development in 1923, but became a permanent fixture after it became a popular landmark.
- In 1980, a baby named James Brady was thrown from a burning building and landed in the arms of a passerby, who caught him and saved his life.
- In the 1980 Winter Olympics, the American hockey team was able to win the gold medal due to a lucky bounce of the puck that led to the game-winning goal.
- In the 1992 Winter Olympics, a skier was able to win a race after losing a ski mid-run, but was able to continue and finish first.

SLEEP IS FOR EVERYONE...

- There is a rare sleep disorder called "exploding head syndrome" where people experience the sensation of a loud explosion in their head while they are falling asleep or waking up.
- The record for the longest period without sleep is 11 days, set by Randy Gardner in 1965.
- The body's internal clock can be reset by exposure to light, particularly blue light.
- Sleeping on your side is generally the best position for optimal sleep quality.
- Sleep patterns can change throughout a person's life, with older adults generally requiring less sleep than younger adults.
- The term "40 winks" refers to a short nap.
- The average person takes about 14 minutes to fall asleep.
- Sleepwalking has been used as a plot device in numerous movies, including "Step Brothers," "The Simpsons Movie," and "Sleeper."
- The world record for the longest marathon of sleeping is 11 days and 25 minutes, set by American high school student, Randy Gardner in 1964.
- Talking in your sleep, also known as somniloquy, is more common in men than in women.
- The word "nightmare" comes from the Middle English word "mare," which means a female evil spirit or demon.
- Elephants are the only other mammals besides humans that are known to experience rapid eye movement (REM) sleep.
- Some people experience sleep paralysis, a condition where they are unable to move or speak while they are transitioning into or out of sleep.

- Some people experience sleep-related eating disorder, where they get up during the night and eat food without being fully awake or conscious.
- Some people experience sleep sex, also known as sexsomnia, where they engage in sexual behaviors during sleep without being fully aware or conscious.
- Ancient Greeks believed that sleep was a time when the soul could escape the body and interact with the gods and the dead.
- In medieval times, sleep was seen as a necessary evil, and many people believed that too much sleep was a sign of laziness or moral decay.
- During the Industrial Revolution, sleep was seen as a waste of time, and people were encouraged to work long hours and get as little sleep as possible.
- In the 1960s and 1970s, the countercultural movement celebrated sleep as a way to escape the constraints of society and experience new forms of consciousness.
- In ancient Rome, sleep was seen as a luxury, and wealthy citizens would often take long naps during the day.

PERSONAL HYGIENE

- In Ancient Rome, urine was used as a mouthwash because it was believed to have antibacterial properties.
- In the 18th century, it was fashionable to have a beauty mark on the face, and people would use mouse skin to create the effect.
- The average person will spend about six months of their life brushing their teeth.
- The ancient Greeks used to clean their teeth with a mixture of iron rust and coral powder.
- The Aztecs used to brush their teeth with a mixture of salt and charcoal.
- The ancient Egyptians used to use a type of toothpaste made from ox hooves and eggshells.
- In ancient China, people would use black sesame seeds to clean their teeth.
- The average person will spend about three months of their life flossing their teeth.
- The ancient Egyptians used to shave their eyebrows and hairline to protect against lice.
- In the Middle Ages, people believed that bad odors spread disease, so they would carry pomanders (a type of fragrant ball) to ward off illness.
- A study has found that a typical office keyboard can carry more bacteria than a toilet seat.
- During the Elizabethan era, women would use lead-based makeup to make their skin look paler, which could cause skin damage and even death.

- In Japan, it is common for people to take a bath every day, often soaking for long periods of time.
- The first deodorant was created in the late 19th century by an inventor named Edna Murphey.
- The average person will produce enough saliva in their lifetime to fill two swimming pools.
- The ancient Romans used to bathe in communal bathhouses, where they would socialize and conduct business.
- The average person will spend about 1,000 hours shaving over the course of their life.
- In some cultures, it is considered polite to burp after a meal to show that you have enjoyed the food.
- The average person will spend about three years of their life on the toilet.
- The ancient Romans used to use a mixture of goat's milk and sulfur to condition their hair.
- In the 17th century, women would use a mixture of snail slime and vinegar to make their skin look more youthful.

THE STRANGE HABITS OF ROYALTY

- Emperor Caligula of Rome made his horse a senator and would often invite it to dinner.
- Marie Antoinette, the Queen of France, had a habit of playing a game of billiards before bed.

- King Louis XIV of France had a daily routine that involved having his hair and beard groomed for several hours.
- Empress Elizabeth of Austria was said to take two-hour baths every day.
- King Henry VIII of England had a collection of over 2,000 tapestries.
- Emperor Nero of Rome had a habit of collecting rare and exotic animals and would often put on shows with them for his guests.
- King George IV of England had a habit of wearing clothes that were two sizes too small to make himself look slimmer.
- Queen Catherine the Great of Russia was an avid collector of art and had a collection of over 4,000 paintings.
- King Charles II of England had a habit of sleeping during the day and staying up all night.
- Empress Wu Zetian of China was known for her intelligence and would often engage in philosophical debates with her advisors.
- King Gustav III of Sweden was said to be obsessed with coffee and would drink up to 20 cups a day.
- Queen Mary I of England had a habit of wearing a wig to cover up her baldness.
- Emperor Peter the Great of Russia had a fascination with dentistry and would often perform extractions on himself and his friends.
- Queen Anne of England had a habit of eating clay as a way to improve her digestion.
- King James I of England had a fascination with witchcraft and wrote a book on the subject.
- King Louis XIV of France was known for his love of opulence and extravagance, and was said to have taken baths in a mixture of milk and honey to keep his skin soft.
- Queen Victoria of England was known for her strict moral code, and was said to have slept with a photograph of her deceased husband, Prince Albert, under her pillow.
- King Ludwig II of Bavaria was known for his love of fairy tales and his elaborate castle-building projects, including the construction of several fantastical castles inspired by the stories of his childhood.
- King Charles VI of France was known for his bouts of insanity, including his belief that he was made of glass and would shatter if touched.
- King George III of England was known for his bouts of madness, including his obsession with the color purple and his habit of speaking to trees.

ANCIENT CIVILIZATIONS

- In ancient Egypt, cats were considered sacred animals and were worshipped as gods. They were believed to have a spiritual connection to the divine, and killing a cat was considered a serious crime punishable by death.
- In ancient Rome, chariot racing was a popular sport that often led to violent clashes between rival factions. The most famous chariot race was the Circus Maximus, which could hold up to 150,000 spectators.
- The ancient Egyptians believed that the heart was the seat of the soul and preserved it during the mummification process. The heart was considered the most important organ and was weighed against a feather during the judgment of the dead.
- The ancient civilization of the Aztecs in Mexico practiced human sacrifice as a form of religious ritual. Victims were often prisoners of war or slaves, and the ritual was believed to ensure the survival of the world.
- The ancient Greek philosopher Aristotle tutored Alexander the Great, one of history's most successful military commanders. Aristotle's teachings influenced Alexander's later conquests and his approach to governance.
- The ancient city of Pompeii was destroyed by the eruption of Mount Vesuvius in 79 AD and was buried in volcanic ash for centuries. The city was rediscovered in the 18th century and is now a popular tourist destination.
- The ancient civilization of the Olmec in Mexico developed a sophisticated calendar system that accurately predicted astronomical events. The calendar was based on a combination of solar and lunar cycles and was used for religious and agricultural purposes.
- The ancient Chinese invented paper, printing, and gunpowder, among other important technologies. These inventions had a profound impact on the development of civilization and continue to shape the modern world.
- The ancient city of Petra in Jordan was known for its impressive water management system, which included channels and reservoirs. This system allowed the city's inhabitants to survive in a desert environment.
- The ancient Greeks developed a system of philosophy that included the ideas of Socrates, Plato, and Aristotle. These philosophers explored questions about the nature of reality, ethics, and politics.
- The ancient civilization of the Inca in Peru developed a system of record-keeping using knotted cords known as quipus. These cords were used to record information about taxes, property, and other important matters.
- The ancient Egyptians were skilled astronomers and used their knowledge of the stars to develop a calendar system. The calendar included 12 months of 30 days each, with an extra 5 days added at the end of the year.
- The ancient civilization of the Vikings believed in a system of justice known as the blood feud, in which the family of a victim was allowed to seek revenge against

the perpetrator. This system often led to cycles of violence and vendettas that could last for generations.
- The ancient Greeks believed in a system of pederasty, in which older men took younger boys as their lovers and mentors. This practice was controversial even in ancient times and remains a subject of debate among scholars.
- The ancient Mayans believed in a practice known as trepanation, in which a hole was drilled into a person's skull as a form of medical treatment. The purpose of the procedure is still unclear, but it may have been used to relieve pressure on the brain.
- The ancient Egyptians believed in the concept of the soul, which they believed could be divided into five different parts. These parts included the ka, the ba, and the akh, which were believed to be important for a person's survival in the afterlife.
- The ancient Greeks believed in the existence of mythical creatures such as centaurs, cyclops, and minotaurs. These creatures were often depicted in art and literature and were believed to be part of the natural world.

THE WORLD'S MOST UNUSUAL SPORTS

- Sepak takraw, a sport popular in Southeast Asia, is similar to volleyball, but players use their feet and head to hit a rattan ball over a net.
- Chessboxing is a sport that combines chess and boxing. Players alternate between playing chess and boxing rounds.
- Underwater hockey is a game played on the bottom of a swimming pool, with players wearing snorkels, fins, and masks.
- Extreme ironing is a sport where participants iron clothes in unusual or dangerous locations, such as on a mountainside or while skydiving.
- Bossaball is a sport that combines volleyball, soccer, gymnastics, and music. It is played on a trampoline-like surface with a net dividing two teams.
- Yukigassen is a snowball-fighting sport from Japan that involves teams trying to hit their opponents with snowballs.
- Zorbing is a sport where participants roll down a hill inside a large transparent plastic ball.
- Kaninhop is a sport where rabbits hop over hurdles and obstacles with their owners guiding them on a leash.
- Shin kicking is a sport where two participants hold onto each other's shoulders and try to kick each other in the shins until one falls to the ground.
- Elephant polo is a sport where players ride on the backs of elephants and try to hit a ball into a goal.

- Cycleball is a sport where two players ride bicycles inside a small arena and try to score by hitting a ball into a goal with their bikes.
- Caber tossing is a sport where participants throw a large pole called a caber end over end.
- Egg tossing is a sport where participants toss a raw egg back and forth, increasing the distance after each round.
- Hornussen is a Swiss sport where players hit a small puck with a wooden paddle and then try to hit the puck with a whip-like stick before it lands.
- Haggis hurling is a Scottish sport where participants throw a haggis (a type of sausage) as far as possible.
- Cheese rolling is a sport where participants race down a hill chasing a rolling wheel of cheese.
- Extreme pogo is a sport where participants perform tricks on a pogo stick, including backflips and front flips.
- Frog jumping is a sport where participants try to jump their frogs as far as possible.
- Wok racing is a sport where participants race down a snow-covered mountain on woks (Chinese cooking pans).
- Lawn mower racing is a sport where participants race modified lawn mowers around a track.

THE WORLD'S MOST UNUSUAL JOBS

- A pet communicator is a person who claims to be able to communicate telepathically with animals.

- A professional cuddler is a person who gets paid to snuggle with clients.
- A food stylist is a person who is responsible for making food look attractive for photographs and videos.
- A snake milker is a person who extracts venom from snakes for use in antivenom.
- A water slide tester is a person who is paid to go down water slides all day and evaluate their safety and fun factor.
- A pet food taster is a person who taste-tests pet food to make sure it is palatable for animals.
- A professional sleeper is a person who gets paid to test out mattresses and other sleep-related products.
- A storm chaser is a person who travels around the world to study and document severe weather conditions.
- A cheese sculptor is a person who creates sculptures out of cheese for events and displays.
- A hot air balloon pilot is a person who flies hot air balloons for a living.
- A treasure hunter is a person who searches for lost or hidden treasures, such as buried gold or ancient artifacts.
- A professional mermaid is a person who performs as a mermaid for events and parties.
- A mattress jumper is a person who jumps on mattresses to test their durability.
- A dinosaur duster is a person who cleans and maintains dinosaur fossils in museums and other institutions.
- A snake oil salesman is a person who sells fake or ineffective products or services.
- A dog masseuse is a person who massages dogs to promote relaxation and wellness.

CONSPIRACY THEORIES

- Some people believe that the moon landing was faked and that the footage was created by Hollywood.
- The Flat Earth Society believes that the Earth is flat, and that any evidence to the contrary is part of a government cover-up.
- The Illuminati is a secret society that some people believe controls world events and governments.
- Some people believe that the 9/11 terrorist attacks were orchestrated by the United States government to justify going to war in the Middle East.
- The "Paul is Dead" conspiracy theory claims that Paul McCartney of the Beatles died in a car crash in 1966 and was replaced by a lookalike.

- The reptilian conspiracy theory claims that powerful people, such as politicians and celebrities, are actually shape-shifting reptilian creatures in disguise.
- Some people believe that the world is controlled by a group of powerful bankers known as the Rothschild family.
- The Bermuda Triangle is believed to be a place where planes and ships disappear without explanation, and some people believe it is caused by extraterrestrial activity.
- Some people believe that the Holocaust never happened, and that it was all a hoax.
- The Denver International Airport is believed to be the site of a secret underground bunker for the world's elite in case of a global catastrophe.
- The New World Order conspiracy theory claims that a secret cabal of elites is working to create a one-world government.
- The Area 51 conspiracy theory claims that the United States government is hiding evidence of extraterrestrial life at a secret base in Nevada.
- The Phantom Time Hypothesis claims that the years 614-911 AD never actually happened, and that they were fabricated by historians to cover up a dark period in European history.
- The JFK assassination conspiracy theory claims that Lee Harvey Oswald did not act alone, and that there was a larger conspiracy involving the CIA or organized crime.
- The Chemtrail conspiracy theory claims that the white trails left by airplanes in the sky are actually chemicals being sprayed by the government for nefarious purposes.
- The Hollow Earth theory claims that the Earth is actually hollow, and that there is a whole world living inside the planet.
- The Mandela Effect is a phenomenon where a large group of people remember an event or detail differently than it actually occurred, and some people believe that it is evidence of parallel universes.
- The Black Knight Satellite is an object in space that some people believe is evidence of extraterrestrial life, but which NASA claims is just space debris.
- The moon is believed by some people to be a hollow artificial satellite created by extraterrestrial beings.
- The Philadelphia Experiment conspiracy theory claims that the US Navy conducted experiments on invisibility and teleportation in the 1940s, with disastrous results.
- Some people believe that the Titanic sinking was part of an insurance fraud scheme, and that the ship that sank was not the Titanic at all.
- The Roswell Incident is believed by some people to be evidence of a crashed UFO, while others believe that it was just a weather balloon.

- Some people believe that the Loch Ness Monster is a real creature that lives in the Loch Ness in Scotland.

STRANGE TECH HABITS

- In China, people use "air-conditioned pants" that are connected to a mobile app to cool down on hot summer days.
- In Japan, some people wear "LED face masks" that use light therapy to improve skin health and reduce wrinkles.
- A survey found that the average person spends about 3 hours and 15 minutes on their phone every day.
- In South Korea, it's common for people to use "selfie sticks" that have built-in fans to keep them cool while taking photos.
- In some countries, such as South Korea and Japan, it's common for people to use "voice changers" to disguise their voices during phone calls and video chats.
- A survey found that 33% of people use their phones to check social media first thing in the morning.
- In some countries, such as Japan and South Korea, it's common for people to use "noise-cancelling forks" that use sound technology to cancel out the noise of chewing and improve dining experiences.
- A survey found that the most popular type of selfie pose is the "duck face," followed by the "smiling selfie" and the "pouty selfie."
- In Japan, some people use "air purifying necklaces" that use ionization technology to purify the air and improve breathing.
- A study found that some people have "nomophobia," which is the fear of being without their phone.

- A study found that some people experience "phantom vibration syndrome," which is the sensation of feeling a vibration from their phone that isn't actually happening.
- In Japan, it is common for people to use smart umbrellas equipped with GPS tracking to ensure they never lose their umbrella again.
- The average person spends more time on their phone than they do interacting with their family and friends.
- Nearly one-third of all smartphone users say they cannot go more than a few hours without checking their phone.
- The average person spends more time on their smartphone than they do sleeping.
- Experts estimate that up to 8% of the general population are addicted to video games. That's the equivalent of the entire combined population of the United States, Canada and Mexico.
- The average person bing-watches their favorite shows 3-10 hours per week.
- Virtual idols: In Japan, virtual idols have become a popular phenomenon, with fans paying to interact with computer-generated pop stars through chatbots and social media.
- In Japan, AI girlfriends, also known as "waifu" or "girlfriend AI" apps, have become a popular trend. These apps allow users to interact with virtual girlfriends, who can hold conversations, provide emotional support, and even send cute texts and photos.

STRANGE FOOD CUSTOMS

- In Ethiopia, they eat a dish called "Kitfo," which is raw meat mixed with spices and butter. This dish is believed to have healing properties.
- In Italy, they eat "Casu Marzu," a type of cheese that contains live maggots. The maggots help to break down the cheese and make it softer and more flavorful.
- In Russia, they eat "Chernyy Khleb," a type of black bread made from rye flour and sawdust. The sawdust is added to make the bread more filling and to help it last longer.
- In Iceland, they eat "Hákarl," fermented shark meat that has been buried underground for several months. This dish is considered a delicacy and is said to have a strong ammonia-like smell and taste.
- In South Korea, they eat "Sannakji," which is live octopus that's chopped up and served while still moving. This dish is believed to be an aphrodisiac and is also high in protein.

- In China, they eat "Bird's Nest Soup," which is made from the saliva of cave-dwelling birds. This dish is believed to have health benefits and is also very expensive.
- In some parts of Africa, they eat "Termites," which are a good source of protein. They are often roasted and eaten as a snack or added to stews and soups.
- In Spain, they eat "Criadillas," which are bull testicles that are boiled, peeled, and fried. This dish is considered a delicacy and is often served as a tapa or snack.
- In Mexico, they drink "Pulque," an alcoholic drink made from fermented agave sap. This drink has been consumed in Mexico for thousands of years and is considered a cultural tradition.
- In the United States, people eat "Deep-fried Butter," which is often served at state fairs. This dish is considered a novelty item and is not meant to be consumed on a regular basis.
- In parts of China, they eat "Yin Yang Fish," where the fish is deep-fried, but the head and tail are left to move on the plate. This dish is considered a delicacy and is believed to have a unique texture and flavor.
- In some parts of Africa, they eat "Mopane Worms," which are caterpillars that are dried, roasted, and often served as a snack or added to stews and soups. They are also considered a good source of protein.
- In Scotland, they eat "Haggis," a dish made from sheep organs, oatmeal, and spices, traditionally cooked in a sheep's stomach. This dish is considered a national dish of Scotland and is often served on Burns Night, a celebration of the Scottish poet Robert Burns.
- In the United States, they eat "Deep-fried Coca-Cola," which is a popular snack at state fairs. The Coca-Cola is mixed with batter and deep-fried to create a unique snack.
- In some parts of China, they eat "Blood Soup," which is a soup made from animal blood and is often served with tofu and vegetables.
- In some parts of Africa, they eat "Giraffe Meat," which is considered a delicacy and is often served during special occasions.
- In some parts of Asia, they eat "Penis Soup," which is a soup made from animal penises and is believed to have aphrodisiac properties.
- In ancient Greece, they ate roasted mice and considered them a delicacy.
- In medieval Europe, blackbirds and peacocks were popular dishes, often served with their feathers still attached to the skin.
- In 19th century England, jellied eels were a popular street food, with vendors serving the dish to people on the go.

PROCRASTINATION CAN BE USEFUL

- ❖ The filmmaker Stanley Kubrick procrastinated on casting the lead actor for his movie "A Clockwork Orange" until just days before filming began. However, he then discovered the relatively unknown actor Malcolm McDowell, who delivered a groundbreaking performance that became one of the most iconic in film history.
- ❖ Tim Urban, the author of the blog "Wait But Why," procrastinated on writing a TED Talk until a few days before the event. However, he then put in an intense 90-hour work marathon to create the presentation, which became one of the most popular TED Talks of all time.
- ❖ The French artist Edgar Degas was known for procrastinating on his paintings until the last minute, sometimes even waiting until the day before a gallery opening to start a new work. However, this habit resulted in some of his most iconic works, such as "The Dance Class" and "L'Absinthe."
- ❖ A study found that people who procrastinate tend to have higher levels of anxiety and depression, which can lead to other negative outcomes.
- ❖ The famous writer Mark Twain once said, "If it's your job to eat a frog, it's best to do it first thing in the morning. And if it's your job to eat two frogs, it's best to eat the biggest one first."
- ❖ Research shows that procrastinators tend to have lower levels of cortisol, the hormone associated with stress.
- ❖ According to a survey, 20% of people identify themselves as chronic procrastinators.
- ❖ The inventor James Dyson spent years procrastinating on creating a new type of vacuum cleaner, but then had a breakthrough idea while on vacation in the

Caribbean. He spent the next five years developing the technology, and his company now sells the best-selling vacuum cleaner in the UK.

- The writer David Sedaris procrastinated on writing a new book until the publisher's deadline was just a few weeks away. However, he then wrote the entire manuscript in a marathon two-week writing session, and the resulting book, "Dress Your Family in Corduroy and Denim," became a bestseller.

- The comedian Jerry Seinfeld procrastinated on writing a new stand-up routine until the day of a big show, but then improvised a set that became one of his most memorable performances.

- The musician Prince procrastinated on recording the album "Purple Rain" until the day before the studio was due to be shut down for renovations. However, he then recorded the entire album in a single day, and it went on to become one of the most iconic albums of the 1980s.

- The filmmaker Richard Linklater procrastinated on shooting his movie "Boyhood" for several years, filming it in short bursts over the course of 12 years. However, this approach allowed the actors to age naturally on screen, resulting in a unique and critically acclaimed film.

- The word "procrastination" comes from the Latin word "procrastinare," which means "to put off until tomorrow."

- The filmmaker Quentin Tarantino procrastinated on writing the script for the movie "Pulp Fiction" until the last possible moment. However, he then wrote a script that became one of the most influential and widely acclaimed movies of the 1990s.

- The singer and actress Bette Midler procrastinated on preparing for a performance until the night of the show. However, she then delivered a flawless performance that earned her a standing ovation.

- The Nobel Prize-winning author Gabriel Garcia Marquez procrastinated on writing his novel "One Hundred Years of Solitude" for years, but then wrote the entire manuscript in a few months after having a vivid dream about the story. The novel went on to become a masterpiece of Latin American literature.

- The comedian Chris Rock procrastinated on writing the script for the movie "Top Five" until the night before filming was scheduled to begin. However, he then wrote a script that was so good, it earned him a standing ovation from the cast and crew.

- The actress Scarlett Johansson procrastinated on learning to sing for her role in the movie "Lost in Translation" until just a few days before filming began. However, she then put in an intense training regimen and recorded a critically acclaimed soundtrack for the film.

- The author Neil Gaiman procrastinated on writing the script for the movie "Coraline" until the last minute, but then wrote a script that became a box office hit and won an Academy Award for Best Animated Feature.

- The British author Douglas Adams famously procrastinated on writing his novel The Hitchhiker's Guide to the Galaxy by playing computer games. However, this led to him discovering a new game called Bureaucracy, which inspired him to create a new storyline for the book.

CURIOUS WEDDING TRADITIONS

- The average cost of a wedding in the United States is around $33,000.
- The tradition of the bride wearing a white dress dates back to Queen Victoria, who wore a white gown for her wedding in 1840.
- In some cultures, it is considered bad luck for the groom to see the bride before the wedding ceremony.
- The most expensive wedding ever recorded was the marriage of Prince Charles and Princess Diana, which cost over $110 million in today's currency.
- In Hindu weddings, the bride and groom exchange flower garlands as a symbol of acceptance and mutual respect.
- The custom of giving wedding favors to guests dates back to ancient Rome, where couples would give guests small bags of sugar-coated almonds.
- The world's largest wedding cake on record weighed over 15,000 pounds and had 12 tiers.
- In some African cultures, it is traditional for the bride and groom to jump over a broomstick as a symbol of their commitment to each other.
- In ancient Greece, brides would wear veils of yellow or red to symbolize fire, which was thought to keep evil spirits away.
- The tradition of throwing rice at the newlyweds dates back to ancient Rome, where guests would throw wheat to symbolize fertility.
- The world's largest wedding bouquet on record weighed over 400 pounds and was made up of over 200,000 flowers.
- In some cultures, it is traditional for the bride to wear a henna tattoo on her hands and feet as a symbol of good luck and happiness.
- The tradition of the father walking the bride down the aisle dates back to ancient Rome, where fathers would give their daughters away as a form of property exchange.
- The most popular month for weddings in the United States is June, followed by August and September.
- In traditional Jewish weddings, the groom breaks a glass with his foot to symbolize the destruction of the Temple in Jerusalem.
- The world's smallest wedding chapel on record is only 2.5 feet wide and 3.5 feet tall, and can fit only two people at a time.

- The world's oldest wedding ring on record was found in Egypt and dates back to around 2,800 BC.
- In some Native American cultures, the bride and groom exchange eagle feathers as a symbol of honor and respect.
- In Scotland, it is customary for the bride to be "blackened" before her wedding day. This involves being covered in various substances, such as treacle, feathers, and flour, and paraded through the streets.

THE MOST AMAZING GHOST SIGHTINGS

- The White House is said to be haunted by the ghosts of former presidents and first ladies, including Abraham Lincoln and Dolley Madison.
- The ghost of a pirate named Blackbeard is said to haunt the North Carolina coast, where he was captured and executed.
- The ghost of Elvis Presley is said to haunt Graceland, his former home in Memphis, Tennessee.
- The Tower of London is said to be haunted by the ghosts of several beheaded queens and other victims of the Tower's dark history.
- The ghost of a woman named Mary Worth is said to appear in mirrors if her name is repeated three times in a row.
- The ghost of a woman named La Llorona is said to haunt rivers and lakes in Hispanic culture, crying for her lost children.
- The ghost of a young boy named Timmy is said to haunt the Queen Mary, a retired ocean liner turned hotel in Long Beach, California.
- The ghost of a Confederate soldier is said to haunt the Gettysburg battlefield in Pennsylvania, where he died in battle.

- The ghost of a young girl named Samantha is said to haunt the Omni Parker House hotel in Boston, Massachusetts.
- The ghost of a man named Colonel Buck is said to haunt the historic Myrtles Plantation in Louisiana, where he was murdered.
- The ghost of a woman named Sarah is said to haunt the Stanley Hotel in Colorado, inspiring Stephen King's novel "The Shining."
- The ghost of a jilted bride named Julia is said to haunt the Hotel Provincial in New Orleans, Louisiana.
- The ghost of a monk is said to haunt the Tower of London, where he was bricked up alive.
- The ghost of a woman named Lucy is said to haunt the Joshua Ward House in Salem, Massachusetts, where she was executed for witchcraft.
- The ghost of a little boy named Bobby is said to haunt the Edinburgh Castle in Scotland.
- The ghost of a woman named Anne Boleyn is said to haunt the Hever Castle in England, where she lived before marrying King Henry VIII.
- The ghost of a dog named Black Shuck is said to haunt the coast of East Anglia, England, where he is said to have terrorized locals.
- The ghost of a former caretaker is said to haunt the Winchester Mystery House in San Jose, California, where he died.
- The ghost of a woman named Lady Dorothy is said to haunt the Raynham Hall in England, where she was caught having an affair and locked up for years.
- The ghost of a young girl named Molly is said to haunt the Omni Mount Washington Resort in New Hampshire.

THE EVOLUTION OF DATING AND LOVE RELATIONSHIPS

- In the Middle Ages, courtly love was a popular concept that involved a chivalrous knight pining for a lady who was usually married to another man.
- In the 19th century, the concept of dating emerged as a way for young people to get to know each other before marriage.
- In the early 20th century, dating rituals often involved young couples going on chaperoned outings or attending dances together.
- The first recorded personal ad appeared in a British newspaper in the 18th century.
- The concept of speed dating was invented in 1998 by Rabbi Yaacov Deyo.

- The term "catfishing" was popularized by a 2010 documentary and refers to the act of pretending to be someone else online.
- The concept of "friends with benefits" emerged in the 1980s as a way for young people to have casual sex without commitment.
- The first mail-order bride service was established in the United States in the 19th century.
- The first video dating service, Great Expectations, was launched in 1976. The service allowed clients to record video profiles of themselves and browse videos of others, with the hope of finding a compatible match.
- The concept of the "pickup artist" emerged in the 1990s as a way for men to learn how to attract women.
- The first interracial dating website, Interracial Match, was launched in 2001. Interracial Match was founded by a Chinese-American named Sam Oschin, who was frustrated with the lack of options for people seeking interracial relationships online.
- The concept of "swiping" in dating apps was popularized by Tinder in 2012.
- The concept of "ghosting" has become so widespread that it was added to the Oxford English Dictionary in 2016.
- In the 18th century, it was common for young women in England to carry around "love apples," which were actually ornate pomanders filled with sweet-smelling herbs and spices.
- In China, it is customary for a man to present his girlfriend with a bouquet of 99 roses, as the number 9 is considered lucky and represents eternal love.
- In the 19th century, young women in the United States sometimes marked their initials on apples and then baked them, in the hopes that the initials of their future husband would be revealed in the pattern of the seeds.
- A couple in Thailand set the record for the longest kiss in 2013, lasting for 58 hours, 35 minutes, and 58 seconds during a Valentine's Day kissing contest. The previous record was held by a couple in Germany who kissed for 32 hours, 7 minutes, and 14 seconds.
- In medieval Europe, a "jousting tournament" was often held as a way of finding a suitable husband for a young woman. Knights would participate in the tournament, and the winner would win the hand of the young woman.
- In medieval Europe, "bundling" was a common practice in which young couples would spend the night together in the same bed, fully clothed and separated by a wooden board. This was a way of getting to know each other before marriage.
- In medieval Europe, "love contracts" were a popular form of prenuptial agreement that laid out the terms of a marriage, including financial arrangements and the duties of each partner.

- In ancient India, arranged marriages were the norm, and families would often hire astrologers to determine the compatibility of the couple based on their birth charts.

THINK YOU KNOW YOUR PET?

- The fur of a cat's nose is unique, much like a human fingerprint. No two cats have the same nose print.
- Ferrets are known for their playful and curious nature, and they can even be trained to do tricks like a dog.
- A house cat can run up to 30 miles per hour, making them one of the fastest domesticated animals.
- Poodles were originally bred in Germany as water retrievers, and their distinctive haircuts were designed to help them swim more efficiently.
- Pet hamsters can run up to 8 miles per night on their exercise wheels.
- Siamese cats have a unique trait called "temperature-sensitive albinism," which means that the colder parts of their body (such as their nose and paws) are darker in color than the rest of their body.
- Dalmatians are born completely white and develop their spots as they grow older.
- Some cats are born with extra toes, a condition called polydactyly. These cats are also known as Hemingway cats, named after the author Ernest Hemingway who was a fan of them.
- Goldfish can recognize faces, and they have been known to swim up to their owners for a greeting.

- Some parrots are able to learn and use over 100 words, and even understand basic concepts like counting and colors.
- The world's oldest dog on record was an Australian cattle dog named Bluey, who lived to be 29 years and 5 months old.
- Hamsters have cheek pouches that they use to store food, and they can carry up to half their body weight in their pouches.
- Cows can see nearly 360 degrees around them, thanks to their eyes being located on the sides of their heads.
- Rabbits have 28 teeth that never stop growing, so they need to constantly chew on hay or other tough foods to keep their teeth filed down.
- Some turtles can retract their head and limbs into their shell for protection, while others have a hinged plastron (the underside of the shell) that can be closed like a trapdoor.
- Koi are social animals and can form close bonds with their owners as well as other Koi in their pond.
- Rabbits have a unique digestive system that requires them to eat their own feces to extract as much nutrition as possible from their food.
- Cows have a very complex social hierarchy and develop close friendships with other cows in their herd.
- The first guide dog was trained in 1929 to assist a blind World War I veteran, and guide dogs have been helping people with visual impairments ever since.
- The world's most expensive pet was a Tibetan Mastiff named "Big Splash" who sold for $1.5 million in China in 2011.

THE WORLD'S WEIRDEST MUSEUMS

- The Museum of Bad Art in Massachusetts collects and displays artwork that is considered to be bad, kitschy, or unintentionally funny.
- The Mutter Museum in Pennsylvania features medical oddities and specimens, including human skulls and preserved bodies.
- The International Cryptozoology Museum in Maine is dedicated to the study of unknown or mythical creatures, such as Bigfoot and the Loch Ness Monster.
- The Museum of Jurassic Technology in California features exhibits on strange and unusual topics, including tiny sculptures carved from human hair.
- The Museum of Death in California displays artifacts related to death, including skulls, autopsy photos, and execution devices.
- The Museum of Sex in New York City features exhibits on the history and culture of sexuality.

- The Museum of Broken Relationships in Croatia displays objects donated by people who have experienced a breakup, along with stories about their significance.
- The Icelandic Phallological Museum in Iceland features a collection of over 200 penises from different species, including humans.
- The Sulabh International Museum of Toilets in India features exhibits on the history and evolution of toilets and sanitation.
- The Leila's Hair Museum in Missouri features a collection of hair art, including jewelry and wreaths made from human hair.
- The Kansas Barbed Wire Museum in Kansas features exhibits on the history and development of barbed wire.
- The Museum of Bread Culture in Germany features exhibits on the history and culture of bread.
- The Ghibli Museum in Japan features exhibits on the history and art of Studio Ghibli, a Japanese animation studio.
- The Salt and Pepper Shaker Museum in Tennessee features a collection of over 20,000 salt and pepper shakers from around the world.
- The Museum of the Paranormal in Connecticut features exhibits on paranormal phenomena, including haunted objects and ghost sightings.
- The American Museum of Tort Law in Connecticut features exhibits on the history and development of tort law, including famous court cases.
- The Museum of Vampires and Legendary Creatures in France features exhibits on vampire lore and other mythical creatures.
- The International Spy Museum in Washington, D.C. features exhibits on the history and culture of espionage.
- The Meguro Parasitological Museum in Japan features a collection of over 45,000 parasites and parasitic specimens.
- The Museum of Jurassic Technology in California features exhibits on strange and unusual topics, including a display on the history of cats trained to fly airplanes.

PHOBIAS YOU NEED TO KNOW ABOUT

- Anatidaephobia is the fear of being watched by a duck.
- Hippopotomonstrosesquippedaliophobia is the fear of long words.
- Arachibutyrophobia is the fear of peanut butter sticking to the roof of your mouth.
- Pogonophobia is the fear of beards.
- Nomophobia is the fear of being without your mobile phone or being unable to use it.
- Genuphobia is the fear of knees.
- Coulrophobia is the fear of clowns.
- Triskaidekaphobia is the fear of the number 13.
- Chaetophobia is the fear of hair.
- Porphyrophobia is the fear of the color purple.
- Ombrophobia is the fear of rain.
- Ablutophobia is the fear of bathing or washing.
- Xanthophobia is the fear of the color yellow.
- Melanophobia is the fear of the color black.
- Chromophobia is the fear of colors in general.
- Lachanophobia is the fear of vegetables.
- Kakorrhaphiophobia is the fear of failure.
- Hylophobia is the fear of forests or wooded areas.
- Haphephobia is the fear of being touched.

- Gephyrophobia is the fear of bridges.
- Ecclesiophobia is the fear of church or organized religion.
- Dentophobia is the fear of dentists or dental procedures.
- Coulrophobia is the fear of clowns.
- Cacomorphobia is the fear of fat people.

THE HISTORY OF THE TELEPHONE AND MODERN COMMUNICATION

- The first words spoken over the telephone were "Mr. Watson, come here. I want to see you." - Alexander Graham Bell made the first telephone call to his assistant, Thomas Watson, in 1876 in Boston, Massachusetts. Bell spilled some battery acid on his clothing and wanted Watson's assistance. Watson was in another room and heard Bell's voice through the phone.
- The first telegraph message was sent by Samuel Morse on May 24, 1844, from Washington, D.C. to Baltimore, Maryland, and was "What hath God wrought?"
- The first commercial telephone exchange was established in New Haven, Connecticut in 1878 and had 21 subscribers.
- The first public payphone was introduced by William Gray in Hartford, Connecticut in 1889 and cost 5 cents for three minutes of use.
- Bell Labs introduced the first cordless telephone, called the "Pocket Phone," in 1965 with a range of up to 1 mile.
- The first mobile phone call was made by Martin Cooper, a Motorola engineer, in New York City in 1973 on a Motorola DynaTAC phone.
- IBM introduced the first smartphone, called Simon, in 1992 with a touch screen, email and fax capabilities, a calendar, calculator, and world clock.
- The first text message was sent by Neil Papworth, a software engineer, in 1992 and read "Merry Christmas."
- The first video call was made by AT&T between New York City and Anaheim, California in 1970 using a Picturephone.
- Willy Mueller introduced the first answering machine, called the "Tel-Magnet," in 1935 for business use.
- The first email was sent by Ray Tomlinson in 1971 and read "QWERTYUIOP."
- Apple introduced the first emoji keyboard in 2011 with the release of iOS 5.
- Jack Dorsey, a co-founder of Twitter, sent the first tweet on March 21, 2006 and it read "just setting up my twttr."
- Shigetaka Kurita, a Japanese designer, created the first emoji set in 1999 for a mobile internet platform called i-mode.

- Apple introduced the first voice assistant, Siri, in 2011 on the iPhone 4S.
- The first telephone operators were young women known as "hello girls" or "telephone girls" who would manually connect calls using a switchboard.
- Iridium introduced the first satellite phone in 1998 that allowed users to make calls from anywhere in the world.
- The first Blackberry smartphone, the Blackberry 5810, was introduced in 2002 with email, phone call, and internet capabilities.
- Apple introduced the first iPhone in 2007, combining a phone, music player, and internet browser in one device.
- The phrase "long distance" originally referred to calls that were more than 100 miles away, but with modern technology, long distance calls are now rare.

CURIOUS FACTS ABOUT MUSIC

- The song "Stairway to Heaven" by Led Zeppelin is the most requested song on FM radio stations, despite never being released as a single. The song was released on their fourth album in 1971 and has since become a classic rock staple.
- The longest song ever recorded is "The Rise and Fall of Bossanova" by PC III, which has a runtime of 13 hours and 23 minutes. It was released on November 16, 2016, and consists of 13,000 individual samples, taking up 1.2 GB of space.
- The shortest song ever recorded is "You Suffer" by Napalm Death, which has a runtime of only 1.316 seconds. It was released on their 1987 album "Scum" and is considered to be a classic example of grindcore music.
- The world's most expensive musical instrument is the Stradivarius violin, which can sell for up to $15 million. The Italian luthier Antonio Stradivari created the

violin in the 17th and 18th centuries, and only around 600 of his instruments are believed to exist today.

❖ The Beatles hold the record for the most number one hits on the Billboard Hot 100 chart, with 20 songs reaching the top spot. They also hold the record for the most songs on the chart overall, with 34 songs appearing in the top 10.

❖ The song "Happy Birthday" is copyrighted, and the rights to it are owned by Warner Chappell Music. The company earns around $2 million per year in licensing fees, as the song is often used in movies, TV shows, and commercials.

❖ The first music video ever aired on MTV was "Video Killed the Radio Star" by The Buggles. It was played at 12:01 am on August 1, 1981, and marked the beginning of a new era of music television.

❖ The term "heavy metal" was first used in the Steppenwolf song "Born to be Wild." The song was released in 1968 and is considered a classic example of the genre.

❖ The song "Bohemian Rhapsody" by Queen is the only song in history to reach number one on the UK charts twice, first in 1975 and again in 1991. It is widely regarded as one of the greatest rock songs of all time.

❖ The highest-selling album of all time is "Thriller" by Michael Jackson, which has sold over 110 million copies worldwide. The album was released in 1982 and includes hits such as "Beat It" and "Billie Jean."

❖ The Rolling Stones' hit song "Satisfaction" was initially written as a folk song, but the band later changed it to a rock version. The song has since become one of their most iconic and recognizable tunes.

❖ The song "Louie Louie" by The Kingsmen became the subject of an FBI investigation in 1963 due to concerns over the song's allegedly indecipherable lyrics. The investigation found no evidence of obscenity, and the song has since become a classic rock hit.

❖ The world's oldest known song is the Hurrian Hymn No. 6, which was written in cuneiform script in ancient Mesopotamia around 1400 BCE. The song was discovered on a clay tablet in the early 1950s in the ancient city of Ugarit, which is now modern-day Syria.

❖ Beethoven continued to compose music even after he went deaf. He created some of his most famous works, including the Ninth Symphony, while completely deaf. Beethoven began to lose his hearing in his mid-20s and was completely deaf by the time he was 48.

❖ Mozart composed his first piece of music at age five. The piece was called "Andante in C" and was written in 1761. Mozart went on to become one of the most famous composers in history, composing over 600 works in his short life.

❖ The term "jazz" originally meant sexual intercourse in African American slang in the early 20th century. The term was later adopted by musicians to describe a style of music that incorporated improvisation and syncopated rhythms.

- The song "Yesterday" by The Beatles is the most covered song in history, with over 2,200 cover versions recorded.
- The song "Smells Like Teen Spirit" by Nirvana was named after a deodorant brand. Kurt Cobain, the band's lead singer and guitarist, came up with the name after a friend wrote "Kurt smells like Teen Spirit" on his wall. Cobain thought it was a revolutionary slogan and wrote the song based on the idea.
- The famous intro to the song "Sweet Child O' Mine" by Guns N' Roses was created by accident. Guitarist Slash was warming up before a recording session and played the riff as a joke. The other band members liked it and they decided to use it in the song.

THE WORLD'S MOST UNUSUAL TRANSPORTATION METHODS

- In Japan, the bullet train is a high-speed train that travels on dedicated tracks and is capable of speeds up to 200 miles per hour.
- In the United Kingdom, a horse-drawn barge is a long, narrow boat that is pulled by a horse along a canal.
- In Mexico, a camioneta is a small, open-air bus that is used to transport people and goods in rural areas.
- In Vietnam, a cyclo is a three-wheeled bicycle that has a seat in the front for a passenger and is pedaled by a driver in the back.
- In Russia, a hovercraft is a vehicle that rides on a cushion of air and can travel over land, water, or ice. They are often used by the military, particularly for amphibious landings and river crossings.
- In Germany, a beer bike is a pedal-powered vehicle that seats up to 16 people and has a built-in bar for serving beer.
- In Bolivia, a teleférico is a cable car system that spans across the city of La Paz and provides efficient transportation for residents and tourists.
- In Sweden, a skijoring rig is a sled that is pulled by a team of dogs while the rider stands on skis.
- In Indonesia, a bemo is a small, open-air minivan that seats up to 10 people and is used as a common mode of transportation in urban areas.
- In Ghana, a tro-tro is a minibus that is used to transport people and goods across the country's often difficult-to-navigate terrain.
- In Thailand, a longtail boat is a narrow boat with a long shaft that extends from the rear and is used to steer the boat.
- In Brazil, a jangada is a type of sailboat that is commonly used by fishermen along the country's coast.

- In India, a tanga is a horse-drawn carriage that is used for short trips in rural areas.
- In Switzerland, a cog railway is a train that uses a toothed rail to climb steep inclines and provides transportation for people and goods in the country's mountainous terrain.
- The kangaroo jumper is a type of human-powered transportation that involves a large spring-like device that allows a person to jump great distances. It is often used for entertainment and exercise.
- Ostrich carts are a unique form of transportation in South Africa, where they are used to give tourists a ride through ostrich farms. The carts are pulled by ostriches and can reach speeds of up to 60 km/h.

ALIENS AND EXTRATERRESTRIAL LIFE

- Students and teachers at a school in Melbourne, Australia claimed to have seen a UFO and encountered beings from another world in 1966 in the Westall UFO incident.
- The Roswell incident refers to the alleged crash of a UFO in Roswell, New Mexico in 1947, which many believe was covered up by the government.
- The "Wow! signal" was a radio signal detected by astronomer Jerry R. Ehman in 1977, which was so unusual that he wrote "Wow!" in the margin of the printout. It was significant because of its strength, 30 times stronger than background radiation, and its narrowband frequency, which made it an intriguing potential candidate for extraterrestrial communication.
- The Drake equation, named after astronomer Frank Drake, is a mathematical formula that attempts to estimate the number of intelligent civilizations in our galaxy.

- The Fermi paradox, named after physicist Enrico Fermi, suggests that given the high likelihood of intelligent life in the universe, we should have already made contact with other civilizations.
- The Betty and Barney Hill abduction refers to a claimed UFO abduction that occurred in 1961 in New Hampshire, which gained national attention.
- The Rendlesham Forest incident is a claimed UFO sighting that took place in 1980 in Suffolk, England, which is often referred to as "Britain's Roswell."
- In 2004, US Navy pilots encountered a strange object in the sky, which was later released in footage by the Pentagon. The object was reportedly flying at high speeds and performing unexpected movements that challenged the pilots' understanding of aerodynamics.
- 'Oumuamua is an object that was discovered passing through our solar system, which is believed to be the first interstellar object detected by scientists.
- The term "flying saucer" was coined by a journalist to describe the shape of the objects seen during the Roswell incident.
- Kepler-452b is a planet that was discovered by the Kepler Space Telescope, which orbits a star similar to our Sun and is believed to have conditions that could potentially support life.
- The Arecibo message was a radio message sent to a distant star cluster in 1974, which contained basic information about humanity and our solar system.
- The "Phoenix Lights" sighting in 1997 refers to a series of lights seen over Phoenix, Arizona, which were later explained as military flares.
- The "Hessdalen lights" are a series of unexplained lights seen in the sky over Hessdalen, Norway, which have been the subject of scientific study.
- The "Men in Black" are a mysterious group that are often associated with UFO sightings and alien encounters, and have been the subject of books and movies.
- In 1954, a group of schoolchildren in Zimbabwe reported seeing a UFO and alien beings near their school. The incident is known as the Ariel School UFO sighting and has become one of the most famous and well-documented UFO sightings in history.
- The Great Filter is a hypothetical concept that suggests that intelligent life is rare in the universe because there are one or more obstacles that prevent civilizations from advancing to a point where they can colonize other planets.
- In 2017, a mysterious radio signal was detected from a star system called Ross 128. The signal was named "Breakthrough Listen" and is believed to be a possible sign of intelligent life. However, the signal has not yet been confirmed to be of extraterrestrial origin.
- The concept of the "grey alien" is one of the most popular and well-known depictions of extraterrestrial life. This image, which features a small, humanoid creature with large eyes and a hairless body, was first popularized in the 1960s and has since become a staple of science fiction.

- In 1987, multiple people in the Gulf Breeze, Florida area reported seeing strange objects in the sky in the Gulf Breeze sightings.

COMIC BOOKS AND SUPERHEROES

- The character of Batman was inspired by Zorro and Sherlock Holmes, and was originally supposed to wear a red costume.
- Superman's original design was based on circus strongmen, and his iconic red trunks were added to avoid a "naked" look.
- Spider-Man was originally rejected by Marvel Comics for being too similar to other characters, but was eventually brought to life by the persistence of writer Stan Lee.
- Wonder Woman's creator, William Moulton Marston, was also the inventor of the polygraph machine (lie detector).
- The Flash was inspired by the Greek god Hermes, who was known for his speed and agility.
- The X-Men were originally named "The Mutants", but were changed to "X-Men" due to the popularity of the word "X" in pop culture.
- Iron Man's original design was based on the character of Howard Hughes, a wealthy industrialist and inventor. Later, the popular film version was partially inspired by Elon Musk.
- Captain America was created as a symbol of American patriotism during World War II, and was originally depicted punching Adolf Hitler on the cover of his first comic book.
- Thor's original design was inspired by Norse mythology, and his hammer Mjolnir is said to be one of the most powerful weapons in the Marvel Universe.
- Black Widow's original costume included a fur hat and a cape, but was eventually changed to a more practical black jumpsuit.
- Daredevil's origin story involves being blinded by radioactive waste as a child, but gaining superhuman senses as a result.
- Doctor Strange is a sorcerer who uses mystical artifacts and spells to battle supernatural threats, and was one of the first Marvel characters to explore the concept of alternate dimensions and parallel universes.
- The Hulk's transformation from scientist Bruce Banner to raging monster is triggered by anger, and he is one of the most powerful beings in the Marvel Universe.
- The character of Wolverine was originally intended as a one-off villain in a Hulk comic, but was later developed into one of the most popular characters in the X-Men franchise.

- The character of Gambit was created by writer Chris Claremont and artist Jim Lee, and was inspired by the classic card game of the same name.
- The character of Rogue was created by writer Chris Claremont and artist Michael Golden, and gained her superpowers from absorbing the memories and powers of others.
- The character of Jean Grey, also known as Phoenix, has one of the most complex and tragic storylines in comic book history, and is often associated with themes of redemption and sacrifice.
- The character of Cable is the son of Cyclops and a clone of Jean Grey, and is known for his futuristic technology and time-traveling abilities.
- The character of Black Widow was created by writer Stan Lee and artist Don Rico in 1964. The character was initially a villain but later became a member of the Avengers and a popular superhero in her own right.
- The character of Aquaman was created in 1941 and was initially not well-received by readers. It wasn't until the character was reinvented in the 1960s as the king of Atlantis that he became popular and established as a major DC Comics hero.

THE WORLD'S MOST UNUSUAL HOLIDAYS

- "Monkey Waiters' Festival" in Japan: This holiday involves monkeys dressed as waiters serving food and drinks to customers.
- "National Cheeseburger Day" in the United States: This holiday was created to celebrate one of America's favorite foods - the cheeseburger. Many restaurants offer special deals and promotions on this day.

- "International Talk Like a Pirate Day": This holiday was created in 1995 by two friends and has since gained popularity around the world. People celebrate by speaking like pirates and dressing up in pirate attire.
- "Holi" in India: This holiday is also known as the "Festival of Colors" and involves people throwing colored powders and water at each other in celebration of spring.
- Día de la Candelaria" in Mexico: This holiday is a celebration of the presentation of Jesus in the temple and involves traditional customs like dressing up dolls and offering them to the Virgin of Candlemas.
- "Dragon Boat Festival" in China: This holiday celebrates the ancient Chinese poet Qu Yuan and involves dragon boat races, eating traditional foods like zongzi (sticky rice dumplings), and hanging herbs and leaves to ward off evil spirits.
- "Nile River Festival" in Egypt: This holiday celebrates the Nile River and involves traditional customs like sailing on feluccas (traditional boats), eating traditional foods like fiteer (Egyptian pastry), and watching performances of traditional music and dance.
- "Gurning World Championships" in England: This holiday is celebrated annually and involves participants making funny faces to win the title of the world's ugliest face.
- "Chinchilla Festival" in Peru: This holiday is celebrated annually and involves dressing up chinchillas in traditional clothing and parading them through the streets.
- "Night of the Radishes" in Mexico: This holiday is celebrated annually on December 23rd and involves carving and displaying giant radishes to celebrate the Christmas season.
- "Day of the Sea" in Bolivia: This holiday involves blessing miniature boats and setting them adrift in a lake as a form of protection and good fortune.
- "Goose Pulling" in Belgium: This holiday involves pulling the head off a goose while on horseback as a form of entertainment.
- "Easter Bilby" in Australia: This holiday involves the Easter bunny being replaced by a bilby (a native marsupial) to promote conservation efforts.
- "Festa della Madonna Bruna" in Italy: This holiday involves carrying a statue of the Madonna through the streets of Matera and then setting off fireworks to celebrate.
- "Saidai-ji Eyo Hadaka Matsuri" in Japan: This holiday involves a massive scramble for a pair of lucky sticks by participants wearing only loincloths.
- "Tuna Tossing Festival" in Australia: This holiday involves tossing a tuna as far as possible to promote fishing and conservation efforts.
- "Els Enfarinats" in Spain: This holiday is celebrated on December 28th and involves a mock battle between two groups, one dressed as soldiers and the

other as rebels. The rebels try to take over the town hall, and at the end of the battle, flour is thrown to represent the victory of the rebels.

- "Bun Festival" in Hong Kong: This holiday is celebrated annually in May and involves climbing a tower of buns to retrieve a "blessed bun" to bring good luck for the coming year.
- "Puck Fair" in Ireland: This holiday is celebrated annually in August and involves crowning a wild mountain goat as king for three days. The festival includes music, dancing, and traditional Irish food.
- "UFO Festival" in Roswell, New Mexico: This holiday is celebrated annually in July and is a celebration of the town's alleged UFO crash in 1947. The festival includes a parade, live music, and a costume contest.

TV SITCOMS

- In "The Big Bang Theory," Sheldon's catchphrase "Bazinga!" was inspired by a prank Jim Parsons (the actor who played Sheldon) pulled on one of his friends.
- The iconic Central Perk set in "Friends" was inspired by a real-life coffee shop in New York City called The Little Owl.
- The "Seinfeld" finale was watched by 76 million viewers, making it the fourth most-watched television finale of all time.
- In "How I Met Your Mother," Neil Patrick Harris' character Barney Stinson's suits were tailored so tightly that he couldn't wear underwear.
- The theme song for "The Fresh Prince of Bel-Air" was written and performed by Will Smith himself.
- "The Simpsons" has been on the air for over 30 years and has aired more than 700 episodes, making it the longest-running American sitcom.
- "MAS*H" had two different finales - one for the east coast and one for the west coast - because of the time zone difference.
- In "Parks and Recreation," the character of Leslie Knope was originally supposed to be a male character named Ken.
- "The Golden Girls" was originally supposed to be called "Miami Nice."
- The exterior shots of Monk's Cafe in "Seinfeld" were actually filmed at a real-life diner called Tom's Restaurant in New York City.
- The "Full House" house in San Francisco is one of the most photographed houses in the United States.
- The character of Frasier Crane from "Cheers" went on to star in his own successful spinoff, "Frasier," which ran for 11 seasons.
- "The Brady Bunch" was filmed on a set that was only one-third the size of a real house, which is why there are no stairs leading up to the second floor.

- The creators of "South Park" made a deal with Comedy Central that they could do whatever they wanted on the show without any interference.
- The set of "Friends" was designed so that the six main characters' apartments were all next to each other, even though it made no logical sense.
- The character of Gilligan on "Gilligan's Island" was originally supposed to be named Willy, but the name was changed to avoid any potential connotations with masturbation.
- In "The Good Place," the character of Janet was originally supposed to be a man named Jason, but the creators changed the character's gender after D'Arcy Carden's audition.
- The character of Schmidt on "New Girl" was originally supposed to be a minor character, but Max Greenfield's performance was so popular that the writers expanded his role.
- "Schitt's Creek" was created by father and son duo Eugene and Dan Levy, who also star in the show as father and son.
- The character of Ben on "Parks and Recreation" was played by a set of triplets, which allowed the show to work around child labor laws.

HI-TECH INSPIRED BY STAR TREK

- Flip-open mobile phones - The communicator device used by Star Trek characters inspired the design of early flip-open mobile phones.
- Voice-activated interfaces - The voice-activated computer interface on the Enterprise inspired the development of virtual assistants that can be controlled by voice commands.

- Tablets and handheld devices - The personal access display device (PADD) used in Star Trek inspired the development of handheld tablets and other similar devices.
- Heads-up displays - The heads-up displays used in Star Trek inspired the development of augmented reality and wearable technology, such as smart glasses.
- Warp Drive - The warp drive technology used in Star Trek inspired research into faster-than-light travel and advanced propulsion systems, with scientists exploring the possibility of interstellar travel.
- Haptic feedback - The touch-based interfaces in Star Trek inspired the development of haptic feedback technology, allowing for a more immersive and tactile experience in various devices.
- Augmented reality contact lenses - The eye implants used in Star Trek inspired the development of augmented reality contact lenses, allowing for the integration of digital information into the real world.
- Voice Commands - The use of voice commands to control various devices, such as computers and smartphones, was first seen in Star Trek and is now a common feature in many devices.
- Smartwatches - The communicator devices used by Star Trek characters were an inspiration for the development of smartwatches, which can be used for communication and various other tasks.
- Telepresence - The concept of telepresence, which involves remote communication and control of devices, was first introduced in Star Trek and is now being used in various fields, such as telemedicine and remote work.
- Holograms - The use of holograms for communication and entertainment in Star Trek has inspired the development of holographic displays for various purposes.
- Replicator - The idea of a machine that can create objects, food, and drinks from raw materials was first introduced in Star Trek and has inspired various efforts towards creating 3D printing and other advanced manufacturing technologies.
- Medical Tricorder - The handheld device used by Star Trek characters to diagnose and treat various medical conditions has inspired the development of various medical technologies, such as portable ultrasound machines.
- Universal Translator - The ability to translate various languages in real-time, as seen in Star Trek, has inspired the development of various language translation technologies, such as Google Translate.
- Solar Sails - The concept of using solar sails, as seen in Star Trek, to propel spacecraft has inspired various scientific studies and projects exploring the possibilities of this type of propulsion.

UNUSUAL HIGH-TECH WE TAKE FOR GRANTED

- ❖ Touchscreens - The ability to control a device with just the touch of a finger is now considered a basic feature on many devices, but it was once a futuristic idea.
- ❖ GPS - The global positioning system is now integrated into most smartphones, allowing people to easily navigate unfamiliar places and find their way back home.
- ❖ Virtual Assistants - Devices like Siri and Alexa have become a common household feature, allowing users to control their devices, play music, and answer questions with just their voice.
- ❖ Augmented Reality - The ability to superimpose digital information onto the real world is now used in a variety of applications, from gaming to education.
- ❖ Wireless Charging - The convenience of being able to charge a device without plugging it in is now taken for granted, but it was once considered a luxury.
- ❖ Streaming Services - From music to movies, streaming services have changed the way people consume entertainment, and are now considered a staple in many households.
- ❖ Face Recognition Technology - The ability to unlock a device or access secure information using just one's face is now commonplace, but was once considered futuristic.
- ❖ Drones - The ability to remotely control flying devices for various purposes, from aerial photography to delivery services, is now a growing industry.
- ❖ Artificial Intelligence - The integration of AI into various devices and systems is now considered a normal aspect of technology, but it was once the stuff of science fiction.
- ❖ The Internet of Things (IoT) - The interconnectedness of devices, allowing them to communicate and exchange data with each other, is now an everyday part of modern technology but was once a novel idea.
- ❖ Voice-controlled Home Automation - The ability to control lighting, temperature, and other aspects of your home with just your voice is now a common feature in many smart homes.
- ❖ Cloud Computing - The idea of accessing information and applications from anywhere in the world via the internet is now a widely accepted concept, but was once revolutionary.
- ❖ Wearable Technology - The integration of technology into wearable devices, such as smartwatches and fitness trackers, is now an everyday part of life for many people.
- ❖ Big Data Analytics - The ability to collect, process, and analyze vast amounts of data to make informed decisions is now a critical part of many industries.

- Autonomous Cars - The development of self-driving cars, which can navigate roads and make decisions on their own, is now a growing industry, but was once considered a futuristic idea.
- 3D Printing - The ability to create physical objects from digital designs using a 3D printer is now widely used in various industries, from medicine to manufacturing.
- Virtual Reality - The ability to experience a simulated environment as if it were real is now used for gaming, education, and even therapy.
- Blockchain Technology - The use of decentralized ledger technology, originally developed for cryptocurrency, is now being applied in various industries, from finance to supply chain management.
- Robots in Manufacturing - The use of robots in the manufacturing process, for tasks such as assembly and inspection, is now a common practice, but was once considered futuristic.
- Hyperloop Transportation - The idea of a high-speed, tube-based transportation system that can move passengers and cargo at speeds of over 700 mph is now being developed, but was once considered a pipe dream.

VIDEO GAMING

- The first video game ever created was called "Tennis for Two" and was played on an oscilloscope in 1958. It was created by physicist William Higinbotham to entertain visitors at a lab's open house. The game was very simple, using only two knobs to control the movement of a small dot on a screen that represented a tennis ball.
- The iconic character of Mario was originally named Jumpman and first appeared in the game "Donkey Kong." Mario was later named after the landlord of the building where Nintendo of America was headquartered at the time.
- The popular game "Minecraft" was created by Markus "Notch" Persson in just six days. The game was first released in 2011 and has since become one of the best-selling video games of all time, with over 200 million copies sold.
- The highest-grossing entertainment product ever made is the video game "Grand Theft Auto V." The game has generated over $6 billion in revenue since its release in 2013.
- The popular game "Pac-Man" was originally named "Puck Man," but the name was changed to avoid vandals changing the "P" to an "F." The game was first released in 1980 and quickly became a pop culture phenomenon.
- The popular game "Sonic the Hedgehog" was originally designed to be a rabbit. The game's creators eventually settled on a hedgehog because they thought it was a more relatable and appealing character.

- The first video game to feature a female protagonist was "Ms. Pac-Man" in 1982. The game was developed as a sequel to "Pac-Man" and allowed players to control a female character for the first time in video game history.
- The popular game "League of Legends" has over 100 million active players each month. The game's popularity has led to the creation of a professional esports league, with players competing for millions of dollars in prize money.
- The game "Angry Birds" was first released in 2009 and has been downloaded over three billion times. The game's simple gameplay and charming characters have made it a favorite among casual gamers.
- The first video game to feature a power-up was "Mario Bros." in 1983. The game's power-up was a mushroom that made Mario grow in size and gave him the ability to break bricks with his head.
- The popular game "The Sims" allows players to create and control virtual people, including their daily routines, social interactions, and even their personal hygiene. The game has been criticized for promoting materialism and shallow values.
- The game "Mortal Kombat" was so violent that it led to the creation of the Entertainment Software Rating Board, a self-regulatory body that rates video games based on their content. The game's creators were also forced to censor the game's violence in order to avoid government intervention.
- The popular game "Animal Crossing" has a built-in feature that allows players to write letters to their future selves. The letters are saved in the game and can be read up to a year later, providing a unique way to document personal growth and reflection.
- The game "Pong" was so popular that it led to a shortage of quarters in many parts of the United States. The game was so addictive that people would wait in line for hours just to play a few rounds.
- The game "Mega Man" was originally going to be called "Rock Man," but the name was changed for the American market to avoid confusion with the rock music genre.
- The game "Mario Kart" has been used in studies to investigate the effects of video games on driving skills. Researchers have found that playing Mario Kart can improve reaction time and spatial awareness, which may translate to improved driving abilities in real life.
- The popular game "Fortnite" has been used for virtual concerts and events, including a concert by rapper Travis Scott that attracted over 12 million players in 2020.
- The popular game "Mortal Kombat" was originally going to be based on Jean-Claude Van Damme's movie "Bloodsport." The game's creators eventually decided to create their own characters and storylines, leading to the creation of one of the most iconic fighting game franchises in history.

- The first video game console to use CDs instead of cartridges was the Sony PlayStation in 1994. The use of CDs allowed for higher-capacity games and better graphics and sound.

BOARD GAMES AIN'T BORING!

- The board game Clue was originally called "Murder!" when it was first released in 1949. The game's original weapons included a bomb and a syringe, but they were later replaced with the more traditional knife, rope, and revolver.
- The original version of Monopoly was designed in 1903 by a woman named Elizabeth Magie, who was a follower of economist Henry George. Magie created the game to teach people about the problems with monopolies and the benefits of land taxation.
- In the board game Risk, the maximum number of armies a player can have is 999. This has led to some players creating elaborate strategies to reach the maximum number of armies.
- The popular board game Scrabble was invented by an unemployed architect named Alfred Mosher Butts during the Great Depression. Butts spent years refining the game's design and was eventually able to sell the rights to the game to the company that would become Milton Bradley.
- The game of Chess was once considered a form of sorcery and was banned by the Catholic Church in the Middle Ages. The church viewed the game as a distraction from religious duties and believed that the movement of the pieces had occult significance.
- The board game Stratego was originally created in the Netherlands in the early 20th century and was used as a teaching tool for military strategy. The game's creator, Jacques Johan Baron de Man, was a retired officer in the Dutch army.

- The game of Go, which originated in China over 2,500 years ago, is considered to be one of the oldest board games still played today. The game is known for its simple rules and complex strategies, and is considered by many to be a test of intelligence and intuition.
- The board game Settlers of Catan was designed in 1995 by a German board game designer named Klaus Teuber. The game's innovative mechanics and emphasis on strategy helped it become one of the most popular board games in the world.
- The game of Backgammon is one of the oldest board games in the world, with origins dating back to ancient Persia. The game's name comes from the Middle English word "gamen" which means "game," and the Old English word "bacan" which means "to back."
- The game of Checkers, also known as Draughts, is believed to have originated in ancient Egypt over 5,000 years ago. The game was played on a board that was similar to modern-day chessboards, and was a favorite of pharaohs and other rulers.
- The board game Pictionary was invented in the 1980s by a man named Robert Angel. The game's unique concept, which involves drawing pictures to convey words or phrases, has made it a popular party game for decades.
- During World War II, the US Navy used a version of Battleship as a training tool for its recruits. The game helped teach sailors about ship identification and tactics, and was used to help prepare them for combat.
- In the game of Monopoly, the most landed-on property is Illinois Avenue, followed closely by "Go" and "Jail." Players are also more likely to land on properties that are close to the "Go to Jail" space.
- In the game of Scrabble, the highest-scoring word possible is "oxyphenbutazone," which is worth 1,778 points. The word is a type of nonsteroidal anti-inflammatory drug.
- In the game of Jenga, the world record for the highest tower ever built is 40 complete levels with a total of 816 blocks. The record was set in 1985 by Robert Grebler and was recognized by the Guinness World Records.
- The game of Snakes and Ladders, also known as Chutes and Ladders, is believed to have originated in ancient India. The game was used as a tool to teach children about karma and the concept of good and evil.
- In the game of Hungry Hungry Hippos, the hippos were originally made out of marbles. The marbles were replaced with plastic hippos in the 1970s to make the game safer for children to play.
- The game of Operation was invented in the 1960s by a man named John Spinello. Spinello sold the rights to the game for just $500, and has since regretted the decision.
- In the game of Yahtzee, the probability of rolling a Yahtzee (five of a kind) on any given turn is 0.08%, or 1 in 1,296. The probability of rolling a Yahtzee on the first turn is even lower, at 0.00077%, or 1 in 129,600.

THE WORLD'S MOST UNUSUAL NATURAL WONDERS

- The Giant's Causeway in Northern Ireland is a UNESCO World Heritage Site made up of 40,000 hexagonal basalt columns that were formed by volcanic activity over 60 million years ago. The tallest of these columns reaches 12 meters in height, and they all fit perfectly together like a puzzle.
- The Door to Hell in Turkmenistan is a natural gas crater that has been burning continuously for over 50 years. It was created in 1971 when Soviet geologists accidentally drilled into a cavern filled with natural gas, causing the ground to collapse and creating the fiery pit.
- The Great Blue Hole in Belize is a massive underwater sinkhole that is over 300 meters wide and 125 meters deep. It was formed during the last ice age, when sea levels were much lower, and was later discovered by Jacques Cousteau in the 1970s.
- The Fly Geyser in Nevada, USA is a colorful hot spring that has been shaped over time by mineral deposits. It is located on private property but can be seen from a nearby road, and the vibrant colors are due to the presence of thermophilic algae and bacteria.
- The Reed Flute Cave in China is a limestone cave that is filled with colorful stalactites and stalagmites, as well as underground rivers and lakes. It has been a popular tourist destination for over 1,200 years, and was named after the reeds that grow outside the cave, which can be used to make flutes.
- The Salar de Uyuni in Bolivia is the world's largest salt flat, spanning over 10,000 square kilometers. It is so flat that it is used to calibrate satellite imagery, and during the rainy season, it turns into the world's largest mirror, reflecting the sky above.
- The Tsingy de Bemaraha in Madagascar is a national park filled with sharp limestone formations that resemble a forest of stone. The name "tsingy" means "walking on tiptoes," as visitors must navigate carefully through the sharp and jagged formations.
- The Waitomo Glowworm Caves in New Zealand are home to a species of bioluminescent insects that light up the cave like a starry night sky. The glowworms create a blue-green light that is used to attract prey, and visitors can take boat tours through the caves to see the magical spectacle.
- The Blue Lagoon in Iceland is a geothermal spa with bright blue water that is rich in minerals, including silica and sulfur. The water is heated naturally by geothermal activity, and the high mineral content is said to be good for the skin.
- The Zhangjiajie National Forest Park in China inspired the floating mountains in the movie Avatar. The park is filled with towering quartzite sandstone pillars, some of which reach over 1,000 meters in height, and visitors can take a glass elevator up to the top for stunning views.

- ❖ The Painted Hills in Oregon, USA are brightly colored hills that have been shaped by thousands of years of erosion and volcanic activity. The hills are made up of layers of volcanic ash, clay, and minerals that have been exposed by wind and water, creating a stunning display of colors.
- ❖ The Chocolate River in Canada is a river that appears to be chocolate-colored due to natural tannins from the surrounding forest. The river is actually the Miramichi River in New Brunswick, and is a popular destination for salmon fishing.
- ❖ The Baatara Gorge in Lebanon is a canyon with a waterfall that drops through a sinkhole, creating a unique natural bridge. The bridge is known as the "Three Bridges Chasm" and is a popular spot for hikers and adventure-seekers.

THE WORLD'S MOST UNUSUAL NATURAL CREATURES

- ❖ The Electric Eel is a type of fish that can generate electric shocks of up to 600 volts to stun prey or defend itself from predators. It is not actually an eel, but is related to catfish and carp.
- ❖ The Venus Flytrap is a carnivorous plant that can snap shut its leaves in a fraction of a second to catch insects. It uses small hairs on its leaves to sense the presence of prey, and once triggered, the leaves will close and the plant will digest the insect.
- ❖ The Blobfish is a deep-sea fish that has a gelatinous, almost blob-like appearance due to its lack of bones and muscles. It is often described as one of the ugliest animals in the world, and it lives at depths of up to 1,200 meters.
- ❖ The Pistol Shrimp is a tiny crustacean that has a claw that can snap shut at speeds of up to 100 kilometers per hour, creating a loud "pop" sound and a shockwave

- that can stun or kill its prey. The sound is so loud that it can also be used to communicate with other shrimp.
- The Corpse Flower is a rare plant that emits a foul odor similar to rotting flesh when it blooms. The smell is used to attract pollinators such as flies and beetles, which are attracted to the odor of decaying flesh.
- The Sea Pen is a soft coral that resembles a feather or a quill. It is named for its resemblance to an old-fashioned pen, and it can retract into its own body for protection.
- The Hairy Frog is a species of frog that has sharp, bony claws that it can push through its skin to use as a weapon against predators. The claws are retracted when not in use, and the frog's skin grows around them to prevent infection.
- The Saiga Antelope is a strange-looking antelope with a long, tubular nose that resembles a trunk. The nose is used to filter out dust and warm up cold air during the winter months.
- The Star-Nosed Mole is a small mole with a bizarre nose that has 22 fleshy, pink tentacles that it uses to feel its way around in the dark. The tentacles are covered in thousands of tiny sensory receptors that help the mole detect prey such as insects and worms.
- The Axolotl is a salamander that has the unique ability to regrow its limbs and even parts of its spinal cord. It can also regenerate damaged organs such as its heart and lungs.

THE ART WORLD

- The world's oldest known painting is a red hand stencil found in a cave in Spain, estimated to be over 64,000 years old. This ancient artwork shows that humans have been creating art for tens of thousands of years.
- The Mona Lisa was stolen from the Louvre in 1911 and was missing for two years before being recovered. The theft and subsequent return of this iconic painting made it even more famous than it already was.
- Vincent van Gogh only sold one painting during his lifetime, and it was to his brother's friend. Despite his lack of commercial success during his lifetime, Van Gogh is now considered one of the greatest artists of all time.
- Pablo Picasso created over 50,000 artworks in his lifetime. This incredible output of work shows Picasso's dedication to his craft and his lifelong passion for creating art.
- The Great Wave off Kanagawa by Hokusai is one of the most famous Japanese prints and depicts a tsunami wave. This striking image has become an icon of Japanese art and culture.
- Leonardo da Vinci's painting The Last Supper took over four years to complete and was painted directly onto the wall of the Santa Maria delle Grazie church in

Milan, Italy. This enormous work of art measures over 15 feet tall and 28 feet wide.

❖ The painting Starry Night by Vincent van Gogh is said to have been inspired by his view from the window of his asylum room. The swirling, dreamlike quality of the painting reflects Van Gogh's mental state at the time.

❖ The sculpture of a urinating boy, known as Manneken Pis, is a famous landmark in Brussels, Belgium. The sculpture has been the subject of various legends and is dressed in different costumes for special occasions.

❖ The painting The Persistence of Memory by Salvador Dali has inspired many works of popular culture, including the cartoon character SpongeBob SquarePants, whose face resembles one of the melting watches in the painting.

❖ The artist Banksy once secretly installed a booth in New York's Central Park that offered "spray art" for $60, but the booth was shut down by police after only a few hours.

❖ The artist Jeff Koons once created a sculpture of Michael Jackson and his pet monkey Bubbles that sold for over $5 million at auction.

❖ The art of glassblowing was once considered a highly secretive trade, with glassblowers guarding their techniques and recipes closely.

❖ The painting The Birth of Venus by Sandro Botticelli was inspired by the writings of the ancient Greek poet Hesiod, who wrote about the goddess emerging from the sea foam.

❖ The art of quilting was once used as a way for slaves to communicate secretly, with patterns and colors used to convey messages about the Underground Railroad.

❖ The painting The Garden of Earthly Delights by Hieronymus Bosch is a triptych, which means it consists of three panels that can be folded together. The painting is known for its fantastical and bizarre imagery, which includes many strange creatures and objects.

❖ The painting The Night Watch by Rembrandt features a group of soldiers, but the painting is not actually set at night. The title was given to the painting because of its dark background, which makes the figures stand out more.

❖ The art of kintsugi involves repairing broken pottery using a mixture of lacquer and gold dust. The repaired object is considered more beautiful and valuable than the original, and it is often used as a symbol of resilience and strength.

❖ The auction of the painting Salvator Mundi by Leonardo da Vinci in 2017, which sold for a record-breaking $450 million caused great controversy when it was later revealed to be in poor condition and possibly not painted by the artist himself.

❖ The depiction of Muhammad in cartoons published in the Danish newspaper Jyllands-Posten in 2005, led to protests and violence around the world.

UNUSUAL LAWS AROUND THE WORLD

- In Illinois, it is illegal to give a lighted cigar to a pet.
- In Thailand, it is illegal to leave your house without wearing underwear. The law was passed to promote good hygiene and prevent people from going nude in public.
- In France, it is illegal to name a pig "Napoleon." The law was passed in the 19th century to protect the reputation of the French emperor.
- In Samoa, it is illegal to forget your wife's birthday. The law is designed to promote family values and ensure that husbands remember important dates.
- In Japan, it is illegal to be overweight. The law, which was introduced in 2009, requires men and women between the ages of 40 and 75 to maintain a waistline below a certain measurement.
- In Switzerland, it is illegal to flush a toilet after 10pm. The law is designed to prevent noise disturbances at night.
- In Denmark, it is illegal to start a car without first checking for sleeping children underneath. The law was introduced to prevent tragic accidents.
- In Singapore, it is illegal to chew gum. The law was introduced in 1992 to prevent gum from being discarded on streets and public spaces.
- In Saudi Arabia, it is illegal to sell cats and dogs as pets. The law is designed to promote the keeping of animals for work and hunting purposes only.
- In Italy, it is illegal to die without a will. The law is designed to prevent disputes over inheritance.
- In England, it is illegal to beat or shake any carpet or rug in the streets. The law dates back to the 1800s and was designed to prevent the spread of dust and dirt.

- In Canada, it is illegal to pay for items with too many coins. The law is designed to prevent businesses from being overwhelmed with loose change.
- In Greece, it is illegal to wear high heels to historical sites. The law was introduced to prevent damage to ancient monuments and artifacts.
- In China, it is illegal to reincarnate without government permission. The law was introduced to prevent Tibetan monks from reincarnating outside of Chinese control.
- In South Africa, it is illegal to own more than 50 kilograms of potatoes. The law was introduced to prevent hoarding and black market sales.
- In Australia, it is illegal to walk on the right-hand side of a footpath. The law is designed to promote pedestrian safety and prevent collisions.
- In Israel, it is illegal to bring bears to the beach. The law was introduced to prevent dangerous encounters between bears and humans.
- In Germany, it is illegal to run out of gas on the Autobahn. The law is designed to prevent accidents and traffic congestion.
- In India, it is illegal to fly a kite without a permit. The law was introduced to prevent kite flying accidents and damage to power lines.
- In the United Arab Emirates, it is illegal to display public affection. The law is designed to promote conservative values and prevent public displays of intimacy.
- In Alabama, it is illegal to wear a fake mustache in church that causes laughter.
- In Arizona, it is illegal for donkeys to sleep in bathtubs.
- In California, it is illegal to whistle for a lost canary before 7 am.
- In Georgia, it is illegal to tie a giraffe to a telephone pole or street lamp.

DÉJÀ VU ALL OVER AGAIN...

- Studies suggest that women are more likely to experience Déjà vu than men.
- People who suffer from epilepsy are more likely to experience Déjà vu than the general population.
- In some cases, Déjà vu can be a symptom of a medical condition, such as a brain tumor or migraine.
- Deja Vu - This is the feeling of having already experienced a moment that is currently happening, even though it's a new experience. It is thought to be related to a brief misfiring of memory circuits in the brain.
- Synesthesia - This is a condition where the brain blends together different senses, such as seeing colors when hearing music or tasting shapes. It is thought to be caused by unusual connections between the brain's sensory regions.

- Phantom Limb Syndrome - This is the sensation of still feeling pain, pressure, or even movement in a limb that has been amputated. It is thought to be caused by the brain's sensory map, which has not adjusted to the loss of the limb.
- Capgras Delusion - This is the belief that a loved one, such as a spouse or family member, has been replaced by an imposter. It is thought to be caused by a malfunction in the brain's emotional processing system.
- Body Dysmorphia - This is the condition where a person has a distorted view of their own body, often thinking that they are much larger or smaller than they actually are. It is thought to be caused by a complex interplay of psychological, social, and cultural factors.
- Tardive Dyskinesia - This is a condition where a person experiences involuntary movements, such as twitching or grimacing, as a side effect of long-term use of certain medications. It is thought to be caused by changes in the brain's dopamine receptors.
- Blindsight - People with blindsight are able to sense and react to objects in their visual field, even though they cannot consciously see them.
- Autoscopy - People with autoscopy may experience seeing their own body from a vantage point outside of themselves, as if they are floating above their own body.
- Emotion Contagion - People can unconsciously catch emotions from others, such as laughing when someone else starts laughing, or feeling anxious when someone else is anxious.

CRYPTOZOOLOGY AND MYTHICAL CREATURES

- The Mothman is a humanoid creature with large wings and glowing red eyes that was sighted in Point Pleasant, West Virginia, in 1966 and 1967.

- The Loch Ness Monster is said to live in Loch Ness, a deep, freshwater lake in Scotland. Sightings of the creature date back to the 6th century.
- The Chupacabra is a creature said to inhabit parts of the Americas, particularly Mexico and Puerto Rico. It is said to attack and drink the blood of livestock.
- The Jersey Devil is a creature said to inhabit the Pine Barrens of southern New Jersey. It is described as a kangaroo-like creature with wings and a goat's head.
- The Kraken is a legendary sea monster said to live off the coasts of Norway and Greenland. It is said to be a giant octopus or squid.
- The Wendigo is a creature from Algonquian folklore said to inhabit the forests of the Great Lakes region of North America. It is said to be a spirit that possesses humans and turns them into cannibals.
- The Thunderbird is from Native American folklore said to inhabit the skies. It is described as a giant bird with wings that create thunder when it flaps them.
- The Yeti, also known as the Abominable Snowman, is said to inhabit the Himalayan region of Nepal, Tibet, and Bhutan. It is described as a large, hairy creature resembling a human.
- The Bunyip is a creature from Australian Aboriginal folklore said to inhabit swamps, billabongs, creeks, and waterholes. It is described as a large, amphibious creature with a dog-like head.
- The Mapinguari is a creature from Amazonian folklore said to inhabit the rainforests of Brazil. It is described as a large, bipedal creature with tough, scaly skin.
- The Mokele-Mbembe is a creature said to inhabit the Congo River basin in Africa. It is described as a sauropod-like creature with a long neck and tail.
- The Hodag is a creature said to inhabit the forests of Wisconsin. It is described as a fearsome creature with horns, spikes, and sharp teeth.
- The Loveland Frog is a creature said to inhabit the Little Miami River near Loveland, Ohio. It is described as a bipedal frog-like creature.
- The Flatwoods Monster is a creature said to have been sighted in Flatwoods, West Virginia, in 1952. It is described as a tall, spindly creature with glowing eyes.
- The Beast of Bray Road is a creature said to inhabit the rural areas of southeastern Wisconsin. It is described as a wolf-like creature with the ability to walk on its hind legs.
- The Black Shuck is a creature from English folklore said to inhabit the coast of East Anglia. It is described as a large, black dog with red eyes.
- The Chimaera is a creature from Greek mythology with the head of a lion, the body of a goat, and the tail of a serpent.
- The Gorgon from Greek mythology had snakes for hair and the ability to turn people to stone with its gaze, and was eventually defeated by Perseus using a mirrored shield to avoid looking directly at the creature.

- The Rokurokubi is a creature from Japanese folklore that is said to be a type of yōkai, or supernatural being, that can stretch its neck to great lengths. It is often depicted as being a female creature that preys on humans at night.
- The Ahool is a creature from Indonesian folklore that is said to resemble a giant bat or owl, with a wingspan of up to 12 feet. It is said to inhabit remote jungles, and sightings of the creature have been reported by locals and travelers.

AMAZING GARDENS

- The Hanging Gardens of Babylon, one of the Seven Wonders of the Ancient World, were built by King Nebuchadnezzar II for his queen, who longed for the plants and trees of her homeland.
- The Medici family of Renaissance Italy were great patrons of botany and horticulture, and their famous Boboli Gardens in Florence became a model for European gardens.
- In 16th century England, knot gardens became popular, featuring intricate patterns of low-growing herbs and flowers, symbolizing the interweaving of human relationships.
- The Japanese rock garden, or karesansui, reached its peak of popularity in the Edo period, and was designed to evoke the essence of natural landscapes using rocks, sand, and moss.
- The French formal garden style, exemplified by the Palace of Versailles, was designed to demonstrate the power and wealth of the monarch, with geometric patterns and stylized nature.
- The Royal Botanic Gardens, Kew, in England, was founded in the 18th century and played a key role in the classification of plants and the study of botany.
- In the 19th century, the English landscape garden style became popular, featuring rolling hills, winding paths, and carefully placed trees and other features to create a natural-looking park.
- The formal Spanish courtyard, or patios, were an important part of Andalusian architecture, featuring ornate tiles, fountains, and lush greenery.
- The Public gardens of Victorian London, such as Kew Gardens and the Royal Botanic Gardens, provided a place for city dwellers to enjoy nature and escape the pollution and noise of the city.
- The Mughal Gardens of India were known for their grandeur and beauty, with expansive lawns, fountains, and canals, as well as the use of raised platforms and terraces to create different levels.
- In ancient China, the imperial palace had extensive gardens and parks, including the famous Garden of Perfect Brightness, which covered over 350 acres.
- The Islamic gardens of the Middle East were known for their water features, such as fountains and reflecting pools, as well as their use of geometry and symmetry.

- The Dutch tulip craze of the 17th century, known as tulip mania, saw tulips become one of the most sought-after and valuable flowers in Europe, with some bulbs selling for ten times the annual income of a skilled worker.
- The French Impressionist movement was influenced by the lush and vibrant gardens of Giverny, where Claude Monet lived and worked, and many of his famous paintings feature the gardens and flower beds.
- In the United States, the Victory Garden movement of World War II encouraged people to grow their own food in response to food shortages, and many public spaces, including city parks, were turned into vegetable gardens.
- The garden city movement of the late 19th and early 20th centuries aimed to create healthier and more sustainable urban environments, with green spaces and parks integrated into the design of cities.
- The Garden of Cosmic Speculation in Scotland, designed by architect and landscape designer Charles Jencks, features sculptures, earthworks, and water features that reflect concepts from science and mathematics.
- The Royal Botanic Garden in Sydney, Australia, is the oldest scientific institution in the country, and features over 30,000 different species of plants, as well as a herbarium, library, and research facilities.
- The Butchart Gardens in Canada started as a depleted limestone quarry, but was transformed into a stunning garden by Jennie Butchart, featuring a Japanese garden, Rose Garden, Italian Garden, and more.

LET'S GO TO THE MALL HONEY...

- In 2007, the Monroeville Mall in Pennsylvania became infamous as the site of a mass shooting, which inspired the film "Dawn of the Dead."

- The first shopping mall in the United States was the Southdale Center in Edina, Minnesota, which opened in 1956 and featured a mix of department stores and specialty shops, as well as a food court and indoor parking.
- The advent of the indoor shopping mall in the mid-20th century marked a significant shift in retail culture, allowing consumers to shop in a climate-controlled environment year-round.
- The largest mall in the world is the New South China Mall in Dongguan, China, which covers over 9 million square feet and features over 2,000 stores.
- The West Edmonton Mall in Canada was once the largest mall in the world and featured a full-size roller coaster, a lake with submarines, and a fully-functioning ice rink.
- The abandoned Hampden Township Mall in Pennsylvania was once home to a thriving indoor farm, complete with cows, chickens, and crops.
- The Berjaya Times Square Mall in Kuala Lumpur, Malaysia, has an indoor roller coaster that loops through the mall's atrium and passes over stores and restaurants.
- The Golden Resources Mall in Beijing, China, was once the largest mall in the world, but now stands largely empty, with entire floors and sections unused.
- The Aventura Mall in Miami, Florida, once had a fully-functioning indoor ski slope, complete with real snow and ski lifts.
- The Concord Mills Mall in North Carolina was once home to a massive indoor go-kart track, featuring a multi-level circuit and high-speed straightaways.
- In the 1990s, the Mall of America in Minnesota became a major tourist destination, attracting millions of visitors each year and establishing itself as a symbol of American consumer culture.
- In recent years, there has been a trend towards repurposing former shopping malls into new uses, such as offices, apartments, and community centers, as communities seek to adapt to changing retail trends and demographics.
- The North Star Mall in San Antonio, Texas, is famous for its giant cowboy hat sign, which has become an iconic symbol of the city.
- The Mall at Short Hills in Short Hills, New Jersey, is known for its high-end luxury shops and designer boutiques, and has been referred to as a "shopping mecca" for the wealthy.
- Mall culture, including the "mall rat" subculture of the 1980s and 90s, has been the subject of numerous books, films, and TV shows, reflecting the central role that malls have played in American consumer culture.
- Some people suffer from a fear of shopping malls, known as "chlorophobia" or "enclosed space phobia," which can cause significant anxiety and distress.
- Shopping malls have been the site of a number of high-profile incidents, including mass shootings, gang violence, and even terrorist attacks, raising concerns about mall security and public safety.

- Mall walkers, or people who walk in malls as a form of exercise, have become a common sight in many shopping centers, particularly in inclement weather.

THE SURREAL HUMAN SUBCONSCIOUS

- The subconscious mind processes about 40 million bits of information per second, compared to the conscious mind, which only processes about 40 bits of information per second.
- Subconscious thoughts can influence our dreams, and some people have even trained themselves to control their dreams and use them for problem-solving and creative problem-solving.
- Subconscious biases can impact our decisions and behavior, even if we don't realize it. For example, studies have shown that people are more likely to help someone in need if they're wearing similar clothes or share a similar background.
- Our subconscious mind can perceive and respond to stimuli that our conscious mind is not aware of. For example, a study found that people could accurately predict which color light would be displayed next even though they were not consciously aware of the pattern.
- The subconscious mind has a powerful impact on our health, including our immune system and stress levels. For example, people who experience a lot of stress have been shown to have a weaker immune response.
- The subconscious mind can store memories that we are not consciously aware of, including traumatic memories. This can lead to the manifestation of psychological conditions like post-traumatic stress disorder (PTSD).
- The subconscious mind can influence our behavior and beliefs through subliminal messages, or messages that are below the level of conscious perception.
- The subconscious mind can affect our ability to learn new information and skills. For example, people who are sleep-deprived have been shown to have a harder time retaining new information.
- The subconscious mind can be trained and programmed through techniques like affirmations, visualization, and hypnosis.
- The subconscious mind can play a role in our perception of time, and time may seem to slow down or speed up based on our emotions and experiences. For example, people who have experienced a traumatic event often report that time seemed to slow down during the event.
- Studies have shown that people can actually continue to perform certain tasks, such as typing, even while they are asleep, as their subconscious mind takes over. For example, in a study conducted at the University of Toledo, researchers found that participants who were asked to type out a sequence of numbers while falling asleep were still able to perform the task accurately, even though they were not consciously aware of what they were doing.

❖ The subconscious mind can also play a role in our perceptions of physical pain, as it can cause us to experience pain even when there is no physical injury. For example, people with chronic pain conditions, such as fibromyalgia, may experience pain even though there is no physical injury or damage to their bodies. This is thought to be due to the way the subconscious mind processes and interprets pain signals.

❖ The subconscious mind has been shown to be capable of learning and retaining information, such as foreign languages, without conscious effort. For example, researchers have found that people who are exposed to a foreign language while they sleep are better able to recall and understand the language when they are awake, even though they have no conscious memory of the exposure. Similarly, people who have listened to a language-learning tape while they sleep have been found to be better able to speak and understand the language, even though they have no conscious memory of the exposure.

ADVENTURES IN RADIO

❖ Radio was initially used for point-to-point communication, such as ship-to-shore communication, before being developed for broadcast use in the early 20th century.

❖ Early radio broadcasts were often performed live, with performers and equipment in the same room, leading to a more intimate and immediate connection with listeners.

❖ In the 1920s, radio became a major source of news and entertainment, with the introduction of commercial radio stations and the growth of network broadcasting.

- The first radio station in the United States, KDKA in Pittsburgh, began broadcasting in 1920 and is credited with launching the commercial radio industry.
- Radio played a major role in the spread of popular music, with early radio stations often featuring live performances by local musicians and the introduction of music-focused radio shows.
- During World War II, radio was an important tool for propaganda and psychological warfare, with governments using radio broadcasts to control the narrative and shape public opinion.
- In the post-war era, radio faced increased competition from television and other forms of media, leading to a decline in its popularity and influence.
- Despite this decline, radio has remained an important source of news and information, particularly in developing countries and rural areas where access to other forms of media may be limited.
- In the early days of radio, a number of inventors and engineers, including Nikola Tesla and Guglielmo Marconi, competed to be the first to transmit radio signals across the Atlantic Ocean.
- In the 1930s, a number of mysterious and unexplained radio signals, known as "numbers stations," began broadcasting around the world. These stations transmitted sequences of numbers and letters, believed to be used for secret communication by intelligence agencies.
- In the late 1930s, a number of amateur radio enthusiasts, known as "ham radio operators," began using their equipment to communicate with people around the world, leading to the growth of a global community of radio enthusiasts.
- In the 1950s, the use of radio for military purposes became increasingly sophisticated, with the development of new technologies for radio navigation, communication, and espionage.
- In the 1960s and 1970s, pirate radio stations, which operated outside of government regulation and control, became popular in many countries, providing an alternative to mainstream radio and challenging the status quo.
- The "Philadelphia Experiment" conspiracy claims that the US government conducted a secret experiment in 1943 that involved using radio waves to make a Navy ship, the USS Eldridge, invisible and teleport it from one location to another.
- The "HAARP" conspiracy claims that the High-Frequency Active Auroral Research Program, a research facility in Alaska, is secretly being used by the government to control the weather, communicate with extraterrestrial life, and carry out mind control experiments.
- The "Radio Wave Mind Control" conspiracy claims that governments and other organizations are using radio waves to control the minds of individuals, inducing thoughts and behaviors, and manipulating public opinion.

- The "Mars Radio Signal" mystery refers to a series of unexplained radio signals that were detected by astronomers in the late 1990s, which some believe may have been transmitted by intelligent life on Mars.
- The "Woodpecker Signal" mystery refers to a series of unexplained radio signals that were detected in the late 1970s, believed by some to be related to a secret military project or extraterrestrial communication.
- The "Montauk Project" conspiracy claims that the US government conducted secret experiments in the 1940s and 1950s involving time travel, mind control, and other advanced technologies, using radio waves and other forms of energy.
- The "Dawn of the Dead Radio Broadcast" mystery refers to an unexplained radio broadcast that was received by amateur radio operators in the late 1970s, featuring a repeating message in a foreign language and eerie background noise.
- The "Death Ray" conspiracy claims that governments and other organizations have developed secret weapons that use radio waves to cause harm or death, and that these weapons have been used in covert operations around the world.
- The "Broadcast Interference" conspiracy claims that governments and other organizations are deliberately interfering with radio signals to control the flow of information and manipulate public opinion, and that this interference is the cause of unexplained radio signal disruptions and other anomalies.

THE STRANGEST FEDEX ALTERNATIVES

- In some parts of the world, delivery services have used elephants, camels, and other animals to deliver messages and packages, taking advantage of their ability to traverse difficult terrain.

- Throughout history, homing pigeons have been used to deliver messages, with their remarkable ability to find their way home used to carry messages over long distances.
- In the 19th century, the Pony Express was a mail delivery service that used horseback riders to deliver messages and packages across the United States.
- During World War I, dogs were trained to deliver messages and supplies in combat, and played a vital role in delivering messages between soldiers and headquarters.
- In the early 20th century, airmail delivery services used biplanes and other aircraft to deliver messages and packages, revolutionizing the speed and efficiency of mail delivery.
- In the early 21st century, a number of delivery services have experimented with using robots and autonomous vehicles to deliver packages, such as the Kiva robots used by Amazon.
- In the early days of the internet, a number of early online delivery services used human couriers to deliver packages and messages, such as the original incarnation of Kozmo.com.
- In some parts of the world, delivery services have used bicycles and other non-motorized vehicles to deliver messages and packages, taking advantage of their efficiency and sustainability.
- In recent years, a number of delivery services have experimented with using balloons and other aerial vehicles to deliver messages and packages, taking advantage of their ability to reach remote and inaccessible locations.
- In the early 20th century, a number of delivery services used trained carrier pigeons to deliver messages and packages, such as the French Pigeon Post service, which operated from 1892 to 1934.
- In the early 20th century, a number of delivery services used airships, such as blimps and zeppelins, to deliver messages and packages, taking advantage of their ability to travel long distances and carry large loads.
- In some parts of the world, delivery services have used dogsleds and other sled-based vehicles to deliver messages and packages, taking advantage of their ability to traverse snowy and icy terrain.
- In ancient China, secret messages were sometimes hidden in fans or other everyday objects and carried by messengers.
- In ancient Greece and Rome, secret messages were sometimes written in invisible ink, or encoded using simple substitution ciphers, and carried by messengers.
- In ancient Egypt, messages were sometimes written on papyrus scrolls and carried by messengers.
- In ancient Mesopotamia, messages were sometimes written on clay tablets and carried by messengers.

- In ancient China, messages were sometimes written on silk strips and carried by messengers.
- In ancient Greece, messengers were sometimes marked with tattoos or other signs to indicate their status as messengers, and to protect them from harm.
- In some cultures, secret messages were sometimes hidden in knots on strings, known as "knot messages," and carried by messengers.
- In ancient Rome, secret messages were sometimes written on wax tablets and carried by messengers.
- In some cultures, messengers were sometimes branded with hot irons or other markings to indicate their status as messengers, and to deter attackers from harming them.

THE WORLD'S MOST UNUSUAL BUILDINGS

- The Atomium in Brussels, Belgium is a building in the shape of an iron molecule that stands 335 feet tall and provides panoramic views of the city.
- The Casa da Música in Porto, Portugal is a concert hall with a distinctive, futuristic design that resembles a giant musical instrument.
- The Guggenheim Museum Bilbao in Bilbao, Spain is a modern art museum with a distinctive, flowing design that resembles a ship or a fish.
- The Capital Gate in Abu Dhabi, UAE is a skyscraper that leans 18 degrees to the west, making it one of the world's most angled buildings.
- The Dancing House in Prague, Czech Republic is a building with a unique, undulating design that resembles a couple dancing, reminiscent of Fred Astaire and Ginger Rogers.
- The Crooked House in Sopot, Poland is a building with a whimsical, irregular design that resembles a fairy-tale house.
- The Haines Shoe House in Hellam, Pennsylvania is a house shaped like a giant shoe that was built in 1948 as a marketing stunt for a local shoe store.
- The Cylindrical House in Nagano, Japan is a house with a circular design that provides panoramic views of the surrounding landscape.
- The Habitat 67 in Montreal, Quebec is a housing complex with a distinctive, modular design that resembles a stack of blocks.
- The Stone House in Guimarães, Portugal is a house that is partially carved into a rocky hillside, giving it the appearance of a natural cave.
- The Kansas City Library in Missouri, USA is a library with a unique, bookshelf-lined atrium that resembles a giant puzzle.
- The Cube Houses in Rotterdam, Netherlands are a group of houses with a distinctive, cubic design that resemble giant dice.

- ❖ The Coop Himmelb(l)au Wolf Dürst Britt & Partners building in Vienna, Austria is a building with a unique, angular design that resembles a giant bird in flight.
- ❖ The Piano House in Huainan, China is a building shaped like a giant grand piano, complete with giant piano keys that serve as balconies.
- ❖ The National Centre for the Performing Arts in Beijing, China is an opera house with a unique, egg-shaped design that resembles a giant pearl.
- ❖ The Longaberger Basket Company headquarters in Newark, Ohio is a building shaped like a giant basket, complete with handles.
- ❖ The Thinnest House in Warsaw, Poland is a house with an ultra-narrow design that is just over four feet wide at its widest point.
- ❖ The Church of Hallgrimur in Reykjavik, Iceland is a church with a unique, modernist design that resembles a rocket ship.
- ❖ The Garden of the Gods Visitor and Nature Center in Colorado, USA is a building with a unique, organic design that resembles a giant tree or a series of interconnected caves.
- ❖ The Piz Gloria restaurant in Switzerland, which was built as a revolving restaurant for the James Bond film "On Her Majesty's Secret Service" and is now a museum dedicated to the Bond franchise.
- ❖ The Gasometer in Vienna, Austria, which was originally used to store natural gas and is now a residential complex.
- ❖ The Airplane Home in Costa Rica, which is a house made from a decommissioned Boeing 727.
- ❖ The Can-Can Club in Tokyo, Japan, which was once a strip club and is now a kindergarten.
- ❖ The Church Brew Works in Pittsburgh, Pennsylvania, which was once a church and is now a brewery and restaurant.
- ❖ The Lumber Baron Inn in Denver, Colorado, which was once a lumber yard and is now a bed and breakfast.
- ❖ The W Hotel in Washington D.C., which was once a government office building and is now a luxury hotel.
- ❖ The Dog Bark Park Inn in Cottonwood, Idaho, which is a bed and breakfast shaped like a giant beagle.

YOU WERE BORN TO READ THESE FACTS ABOUT PSYCHICS & ASTROLOGY

- Tarot cards were initially created for gaming and gambling in the early Renaissance period, and were not commonly used for divination until the late 18th century.
- The images and symbols on tarot cards are meant to evoke a specific emotional response and spark the reader's intuition, rather than represent literal meanings.
- The tarot deck is divided into two main sections, the Major Arcana and the Minor Arcana. The Major Arcana cards represent significant life events and archetypes, while the Minor Arcana cards represent everyday experiences and situations.
- Some crystals, such as quartz and amethyst, are piezoelectric, which means that they generate an electric charge when compressed or squeezed.
- Crystals have been used for healing and spiritual purposes for thousands of years, dating back to ancient civilizations such as the Egyptians, Greeks, and Chinese.
- The color of a crystal can affect its energy and properties, with each color having a specific meaning and purpose.
- Many crystals are formed from minerals that are found in the earth's crust, and are the result of millions of years of geological processes.
- Some crystals are so rare and valuable that they can sell for thousands or even millions of dollars, such as the Pink Star diamond, which sold for $71 million in 2017.
- The zodiac signs were originally named after the constellations that they corresponded with, but due to shifts in the Earth's axis, the signs are now slightly off from their original positions.

- The ancient Babylonians are believed to have been the first to develop astrology as we know it today, and they used it for both divination and agricultural purposes.
- There are many different types of astrology, such as Western astrology, Vedic astrology, Chinese astrology, and Mayan astrology, each with its own unique system of interpretation and symbolism.
- The moon is considered to be one of the most important celestial bodies in astrology, as it represents a person's emotions, instincts, and inner world.
- The planet Saturn is often associated with hard work, discipline, and responsibility, and is said to bring challenges and lessons into a person's life.
- The planet Uranus is associated with innovation, rebellion, and change, and is said to bring sudden insights and breakthroughs into a person's life.
- The position of the North Node and South Node in a birth chart can reveal a person's karmic patterns and life purpose.
- The rising sign, or ascendant, represents a person's outward appearance and the impression they make on others, and is said to influence their personality and demeanor.
- The positions of the planets at the time of a major event, such as a wedding or business venture, can be used to gain insight into the outcome and potential challenges.
- Some psychics claim to have psychic animals, such as cats or dogs, that can help them access information or communicate with the spirit world.
- Clairvoyance is a term that comes from the French words "clair," meaning clear, and "voyance," meaning vision.

CAN I BORROW YOUR WHEELS ?

- The world's longest tandem bicycle was over 20 meters long and could seat 35 people. This unique bicycle was built in the Netherlands and was used to promote cycling and raise money for charity. It required a team of riders to pedal and steer the massive bike, which weighed over 3,000 pounds.
- The first bicycles, invented in the early 1800s, were called "velocipedes" and had no pedals. These early bicycles were propelled by pushing off the ground with one's feet, similar to the way a child learns to ride a balance bike. It wasn't until the 1860s that bicycles with pedals were invented and became more popular.
- The world's first bicycle race took place in Paris in 1868 and covered a distance of 1,200 meters. The race was organized by a French cycling magazine and was open to anyone who owned a bicycle. The winner, Englishman James Moore, completed the race in just under three minutes.
- The world's first mountain bike was invented in the late 1970s by a group of Californian cyclists who modified their bikes to handle rough terrain. These early

mountain bikes had wider tires and stronger frames than road bikes, and were designed for off-road use. Today, mountain biking is a popular sport and recreational activity enjoyed by millions of people around the world.

- The fastest speed ever recorded on a bicycle was over 184 mph, achieved by a British cyclist named Neil Campbell in 2019. Campbell set the record on a custom-built bicycle that was powered by a modified motorcycle engine. He rode the bike on a specially designed runway in Yorkshire, England.
- The longest distance ever ridden on a bicycle in one day is over 500 miles, achieved by a British cyclist named Tommy Godwin in 1939. Godwin set the record while attempting to break the record for the most miles ridden in a single year, which he achieved by riding over 75,000 miles in 365 days.
- The first bicycles designed specifically for women were introduced in the late 1800s and featured a lower crossbar to accommodate long skirts. These early women's bicycles were also lighter and easier to maneuver than men's bikes, and helped to promote cycling as a healthy and fashionable activity for women.
- The Tour de France, one of the world's most famous bicycle races, was first held in 1903 and covers a distance of over 2,000 miles. The race is held annually in France and attracts some of the world's best cyclists. The route changes each year and includes challenging climbs, flat sections, and time trials.
- The world's smallest bicycle, created by a German engineer in 2013, measures just 3.54 inches tall and is fully functional. The tiny bike is made from aluminum and weighs just 5 grams. It can be ridden by a miniature figure or displayed as a unique piece of art.
- The world's largest bicycle, created by a team of Dutch engineers in 2018, is over 100 feet long and can seat up to 20 people. This massive bike was designed to promote cycling and sustainable transportation. It is powered by a team of cyclists who pedal the bike together, similar to a tandem bicycle.
- Unicycles have been around since the early 1800s, and were originally called "velocipedes" like their two-wheeled counterparts.
- Unicycles are commonly used in unicycle hockey, a sport similar to traditional hockey but played on unicycles.
- The world record for the longest unicycle journey is over 11,000 miles, achieved by a British cyclist named Ed Pratt in 2019.
- In Japan, there is a unique form of tricycle racing called keirin, in which riders race around a velodrome on motorized tricycles. This popular sport originated in the 1940s and is now a popular form of gambling, with spectators betting on the outcome of each race.
- The world's oldest tricycle was built in 1817 and is now on display at the National Museum of Scotland in Edinburgh. This unique tricycle, known as the "draisine" or "running machine," was invented by Karl von Drais and was the precursor to the modern bicycle.

- In the 1930s, a British inventor named Richard O'Brien created a unique tricycle with a bathtub as the body, called the "Bathcycle." This unusual tricycle was powered by a small engine and was designed to be used on water as well as land, making it a truly unique and versatile mode of transportation.
- In the early 1900s, tricycles were popular among women who wore long skirts, as they provided a more stable and practical form of transportation than bicycles.

SPORTS EQUIPMENT BLUNDERS AND ADVANCEMENTS

- The first basketballs were made of leather and had a circumference of around 30 inches, which was much larger than the standard size used today.
- The first baseball gloves were introduced in the late 1800s and were made of leather and padding to protect the hands of fielders. Prior to this, players would catch the ball with their bare hands.
- The first golf balls were made of feathers and leather and were much smaller than the modern golf ball. They were also much softer, making them easier to control but less durable.
- The first footballs were made of leather and were much softer and less spherical than modern footballs. They were also much smaller, with a circumference of around 28 inches.
- The first modern tennis racket was patented in 1874 and had a much simpler design than modern rackets, with a smaller head and a much smaller sweet spot.
- The first boxing gloves were introduced in the late 1700s and were much smaller and less padded than modern gloves. They were also made of leather and were much less protective than modern gloves.
- The first modern skateboards were introduced in the 1950s and were much simpler in design than modern skateboards, with a smaller deck and no grip tape.
- The introduction of synthetic materials in tennis rackets, which made them lighter, stronger, and more durable than traditional wooden rackets.
- The use of aerodynamic design in golf clubs improved the speed and accuracy of golf shots.
- The introduction of shock-absorbing materials in basketball shoes reduced the risk of injury and improved the comfort of players.
- The use of carbon fiber in hockey sticks made them lighter and stronger than traditional wooden sticks.
- The use of polyurethane in skateboard wheels made them smoother and faster than traditional wheels.

- The use of aerodynamic design in soccer balls improved the speed and accuracy of soccer shots.
- The use of high-tech materials in snowboards made them lighter and more durable than traditional snowboards.
- The metal tennis racket was patented in 1875 and made the sport faster and more intense.
- The golf tee was patented in 1899 and made the sport easier and more accessible to people of all skill levels.
- The aluminum baseball bat was introduced in the 1970s and made the sport faster and more exciting.
- The hockey puck was introduced in the late 1800s and made the sport faster and more exciting.
- The skateboard truck was patented in the 1950s and made the sport more maneuverable and more exciting.
- The synthetic soccer ball was introduced in the 1970s and made the sport faster and more exciting.
- The snowboard binding was patented in the 1980s and made the sport more accessible and more enjoyable.
- Boxing headgear was introduced in the 1960s and made the sport safer and more accessible.
- The golf cart was patented in the 1930s and made the sport easier and more accessible to people of all skill levels.
- The football helmet was introduced in the early 1900s and made the sport safer and more accessible.

AMUSEMENT PARKS YOU WISH YOU COULD VISIT

- The "Nigloland" theme park in France has a section dedicated to the senses, with attractions like a giant nose that sprays different scents.
- The world's first underwater amusement park, "Atlantis, The Palm" is located in Dubai and has a variety of marine-themed attractions and rides.
- The "Suoi Tien Cultural Theme Park" in Ho Chi Minh City, Vietnam, features a giant dragon-shaped water slide and a lake filled with koi fish.
- The "Diggerland" theme park in the UK allows visitors to operate real construction machinery, such as diggers and bulldozers.
- The "Window of the World" theme park in China features miniature replicas of famous world landmarks, such as the Eiffel Tower and the Pyramids of Giza.
- The "Efteling" theme park in the Netherlands is based on fairy tales and has attractions like a dark ride through the story of "Sleeping Beauty."
- The "Everland" theme park in South Korea has a "Lost Valley" area with animatronic dinosaurs and a "T Express" wooden roller coaster.
- The "Hersheypark" in Pennsylvania is known for its chocolate-themed attractions, including a roller coaster named "The Hershey's Kisses."
- "Idlewild Park" in Ligonier, Pennsylvania, was the first amusement park marketed specifically towards African American patrons.
- "Rockaway Beach Amusement Park" in Queens, New York, was a seaside park that operated from 1901 to 1985 and was once the largest amusement park in the United States.
- "Dreamland" in Coney Island, New York, was one of the largest amusement parks in the world at the turn of the 20th century, with attractions like a human aquarium and a shoot-the-chutes ride.

- "White City" in London, England was a popular amusement park that operated from 1904 to 1908, featuring a large central lake and several rides.
- "Crystal Beach" in Ontario, Canada, was a popular amusement park and resort area that operated for 101 years, from 1888 to 1989.
- "Tivoli Gardens" in Copenhagen, Denmark, is one of the oldest amusement parks in the world, having opened in 1843. It features rides like the historic wooden roller coaster "Rutschebanen."
- "Blackpool Pleasure Beach" in Blackpool, England, is one of the oldest amusement parks in the UK and has been open since 1896.
- "Bakken" in Klampenborg, Denmark, is the world's oldest amusement park, having opened in 1583. It features rides like the historic wooden roller coaster "Wild Train."
- The Pleasure Gardens of the Mughal Emperors in India were grand and elaborate parks that were used for leisure and entertainment. People would relax, take in the beauty of the gardens, and enjoy performances, such as music and theater.
- The Versailles Palace Garden in France was a grand and elaborate park used for leisure and entertainment by the French royalty. People would relax in the gardens, take in the beauty of the fountains and sculptures, and enjoy musical performances.
- The Boboli Gardens in Florence, Italy, were a grand and elaborate park filled with sculptures, fountains, and grottoes and were used for leisure and entertainment by the Medici family. People would stroll through the gardens, relax by the fountains, and admire the sculptures and grottoes.

THE SCIENCE OF MEMORY

- Kim Peek, the inspiration for the movie "Rain Man," had a photographic memory and could recall vast amounts of information from books and maps, but had difficulty with daily tasks such as brushing his teeth.
- Ajith Karimpana, a cab driver from India, memorized the entire telephone directory of Mumbai, which consisted of over 180,000 numbers.
- Shereshevsky, a mnemonist studied by Russian psychologist A.R. Luria, was able to remember entire poems and long strings of numbers after hearing them just once.
- "Memory athletes" compete in memory competitions, where they perform amazing feats such as memorizing the order of a deck of cards in under a minute.
- "Eidetic memory" is a rare type of memory where a person can vividly recall images, sounds, or objects after just a few seconds of exposure.
- "Savants" are people with exceptional abilities in specific areas, such as mathematics or music, often despite having lower overall cognitive abilities.

- "Muscle memory" refers to the ability of our muscles to remember movements, allowing us to perform complex motor tasks with ease, such as riding a bike.
- "Flashbulb memories" are memories of the moment and circumstances in which a piece of surprising or emotionally charged news was heard.
- The "memory palace" technique, also known as the "method of loci," is a mnemonic device where information is associated with specific locations in an imagined environment.
- Jill Price, also known as "The Memory Keeper," has a condition known as hyperthymesia, which allows her to recall nearly every day of her life in vivid detail.
- Orlando Serrell was hit by a baseball at the age of 10 and developed an extraordinary ability to recall specific dates, weather conditions, and events that occurred on those days.
- Tamara Lanier sued Harvard University over their ownership of images of her ancestor, Renty, a slave, whom she was able to identify through her memories of family stories passed down through generations.
- Joshua Foer, a former U.S.A. Memory Champion, was able to memorize the order of a deck of cards in under a minute using memory techniques.
- Stephen Wiltshire, an artist with autism, is able to draw incredibly detailed panoramic cityscapes after just one brief helicopter ride over the city.
- Marcel Proust, the French author of "In Search of Lost Time," had a prodigious memory for detail and is famous for his descriptions of sensory experiences and memories.
- Ruth Lawrence is a British mathematician who had an exceptional ability to perform complex calculations at a young age and was able to solve mathematical problems faster than a computer.
- Derek Paravicini is a blind British pianist with exceptional musical memory and is able to play pieces he has heard just once, even years later.
- Jonathan Knight, a British man with synaesthesia, has an exceptional ability to recall the colors and shapes of thousands of words and numbers.

ESP

- Betty Andreasson Luca, an American woman, claimed to have had an extraterrestrial abduction experience and a premonition of the Challenger space shuttle disaster, which was later verified by NASA.
- Ines Ramón, a Spanish woman, claimed to have had a premonition of the 2004 Indian Ocean tsunami, which was later verified by the Spanish Red Cross.
- Paul McCartney, the British musician, claimed to have had a dream about his late bandmate John Lennon, which inspired him to write the song "Yesterday."
- Nonna Bannister, a British woman, claimed to have had a dream about her daughter, who was later found to have been in a car accident on the same road that Bannister had seen in her dream.
- Mary Whiton Calkins, an American psychologist, claimed to have had a dream about a patient's personal life, which was later confirmed by the patient.
- Elizabeth Klarer, a South African woman, claimed to have had telepathic communication with extraterrestrial beings and a premonition of the assassination of John F. Kennedy, which was later verified by historical records.
- Helen Duncan, a Scottish woman, claimed to have had a premonition of the sinking of the HMS Hood, which was later verified by naval records.
- Ingo Swann, an American psychic, claimed to have had remote viewing experiences, including the ability to see the location and activity of a military submarine, which was later verified by the U.S. government.
- Guy Lyon Playfair, a British author and parapsychologist, claimed to have had a premonition of the assassination of John F. Kennedy, which was later verified by historical records.
- Doris Stokes, a British spiritualist medium, claimed to have had a premonition of the sudden death of her son, which was later verified by her family.

- Betty Eadie, an American woman, claimed to have had a near-death experience and a premonition of her daughter's future career, which was later verified by her daughter.
- Peter Hurkos, a Dutch psychic, claimed to have had premonitions of several historical events, including the sinking of the Titanic, which was later verified by historical records.
- Rosemary Altea, a British psychic, claimed to have had a premonition of the 9/11 terrorist attacks, which was later verified by historical records.
- John Edward, an American psychic medium, claimed to have had several accurate premonitions, including the death of Princess Diana, which was later verified by historical records.
- Sylvia Browne, an American psychic medium, claimed to have had several accurate premonitions, including the location of missing persons, which were later verified by law enforcement.
- Ruth Montgomery, an American author and psychic, claimed to have had several premonitions, including the assassination of John F. Kennedy, which were later verified by historical records.
- James Van Praagh, an American psychic medium, claimed to have had several accurate premonitions, including the death of Princess Diana, which was later verified by historical records.
- Gordon Smith, a British psychic medium, claimed to have had several accurate premonitions, including the death of Princess Diana, which was later verified by historical records.
- Tony Stockwell, a British psychic medium, claimed to have had several accurate premonitions, including the location of missing persons, which were later verified by law enforcement.
- Allison Dubois, an American psychic medium, claimed to have had several accurate premonitions, including the location of missing persons, which were later verified by law enforcement.

YOU SEE COLORS WHEN I TALK?

- Vladimir Nabokov, the Russian-American author of "Lolita," had a form of synesthesia that allowed him to see letters and numbers as having specific colors.
- Pharrell Williams, the American musician and producer, has reported experiencing synesthesia, including seeing music as colors.
- Daniel Tammet, a British man with high-functioning autism, has a form of synesthesia that allows him to experience numbers as shapes, colors, and textures.
- Lord Kelvin, the Irish physicist and engineer, had a form of synesthesia that allowed him to see mathematical concepts as colors and shapes.

- Simone Simons, the Dutch singer for the symphonic metal band Epica, has reported experiencing synesthesia, including seeing music as colors and shapes.
- Michael Torke, the American composer, has reported experiencing synesthesia, including seeing music as colors and shapes.
- Vincent van Gogh, the Dutch post-Impressionist painter, is believed to have had a form of chromesthesia, in which he saw colors in response to music.
- Duke Ellington, the American jazz composer and pianist, had a form of chromesthesia, in which he saw colors in response to music.
- Franz Liszt, the Hungarian composer and pianist, had a form of chromesthesia, in which he saw colors in response to music.
- Nikolai Rimsky-Korsakov, the Russian composer, had a form of chromesthesia, in which he saw colors in response to music.
- Hélène Grimaud, the French classical pianist, has reported experiencing synesthesia, including seeing music as colors.
- Tori Amos, the American singer-songwriter, has reported experiencing synesthesia, including seeing music as colors.
- Pat Martino, the American jazz guitarist, has reported experiencing synesthesia, including seeing music as colors.
- Freddie Mercury, the British musician and lead vocalist for the rock band Queen, had a form of chromesthesia, in which he saw colors in response to music.
- Oliver Sacks, the British neurologist and author, had a form of synesthesia in which he experienced numbers as having specific personalities and emotional qualities.
- Scott McCloud, the American cartoonist and comics theorist, has reported experiencing synesthesia, including seeing written words as colors.
- Wassily Kandinsky, the Russian abstract painter, had a form of chromesthesia, in which he saw colors in response to music.
- Synthia Saint James, the American artist and illustrator, has reported experiencing synesthesia, including seeing colors in response to numbers and letters.
- David Hockney, the British painter, has reported experiencing synesthesia, including seeing colors in response to music.
- Shani Rhys James, a Welsh painter, has reported experiencing synesthesia, including seeing colors in response to music and touch.

SURVIVAL MYTHS VS FACT

- "Running away" from a charging bear is a dangerous myth, as this can trigger the bear's instinct to chase. The recommended response to a bear charge is to fight back with anything available and to make yourself as large and loud as possible to scare the bear away.
- "Playing dead" is a common myth about surviving a bear attack, but in reality, this strategy is often not effective and can actually provoke the bear to attack. The recommended response to a bear attack is to fight back with anything available.
- "Sucking the venom out of a snake bite" is a common myth about treating snake bites, but in reality, this strategy can actually make the bite worse by spreading the venom. The recommended response to a snake bite is to seek medical attention as soon as possible.
- "Jumping into cold water to survive hypothermia" is a common myth, but in reality, jumping into cold water can actually worsen hypothermia by causing the body to go into shock. The recommended response to hypothermia is to slowly warm up and seek medical attention.
- "Applying a tourniquet to stop bleeding" is a common myth, but in reality, tourniquets can actually cause more harm than good by cutting off blood flow and leading to the loss of the affected limb. The recommended response to severe bleeding is to apply direct pressure to the wound and seek medical attention.
- "Putting butter on a burn" is a common myth, but in reality, putting butter on a burn can actually make the burn worse by trapping heat and bacteria in the wound. The recommended response to a burn is to run cool water over the wound and seek medical attention.

- "Drinking alcohol to stay warm" is a common myth, but in reality, drinking alcohol can actually worsen hypothermia by dilating blood vessels and causing heat to be lost more quickly.
- "Removing a tick by burning it" is a common myth, but in reality, burning a tick can actually cause the tick to release more disease-causing bacteria into the bloodstream. The recommended response to a tick bite is to remove the tick with fine-tipped tweezers and seek medical attention if necessary.
- "Putting oil on a jellyfish sting" is a common myth, but in reality, putting oil on a jellyfish sting can actually make the sting worse by releasing more venom into the skin. The recommended response to a jellyfish sting is to rinse the affected area with vinegar and seek medical attention if necessary.
- "Rubbing snow on frostbite" is a common myth, but in reality, rubbing snow on frostbite can actually make the condition worse by causing further damage to the frozen tissue. The recommended response to frostbite is to warm the affected area slowly and seek medical attention.
- "Staying still in the water to avoid attracting a crocodile or alligator" is a common myth, but in reality, this can actually make the situation worse by making it easier for the animal to attack. The recommended response to a crocodile or alligator attack is to try to escape and fight back with anything available.
- "Removing a leech by burning it or applying salt" is a common myth, but in reality, these methods can actually make the situation worse by causing the leech to regurgitate into the wound and increase the risk of infection. The recommended response to a leech bite is to gently remove it with a fingernail or tweezers and seek medical attention if necessary.
- "Putting dirt or mud on a wound to stop bleeding" is a common myth, but in reality, this can actually make the situation worse by causing an infection and increasing the risk of sepsis. The recommended response to a bleeding wound is to clean the area and apply direct pressure to the wound.
- "Using mouth-to-mouth resuscitation on a drowning victim" is a dangerous myth, as this can cause water to be inhaled into the lungs and increase the risk of aspiration pneumonia. The recommended response to a drowning victim is to perform cardiopulmonary resuscitation (CPR) and seek medical attention as soon as possible.
- "Applying ice to a sprained ankle" is a common myth, but in reality, applying ice to a sprained ankle can actually make the situation worse by causing further tissue damage and reducing blood flow. The recommended response to a sprained ankle is to rest, elevate, and wrap the affected area.
- "Using leaves or moss as insulation in cold weather" is a dangerous myth, as these materials can cause hypothermia by absorbing moisture and reducing insulation. The recommended response to cold weather is to wear warm, dry clothing and seek shelter.
- "Jumping into a body of water to avoid a wildfire" is a dangerous myth, as this can cause burns, inhaling dangerous gases, and reducing the ability to escape.

- The recommended response to a wildfire is to evacuate to a safe area and seek shelter.
- "Sleeping under a tree to avoid a snake bite" is a dangerous myth, as snakes can climb trees and bite from above. The recommended response to a snake bite is to seek medical attention as soon as possible.
- "Throwing objects at a snake to scare it away" is a dangerous myth, as this can cause the snake to become more aggressive and increase the risk of attack. The recommended response to a snake is to slowly and calmly move away and to seek help from a trained professional if necessary.

HUMANS VS. NATURE

- Prioritize finding a source of clean drinking water: Look for streams, rivers, or other bodies of water, and if possible, boil or treat the water before drinking.
- Collecting rainwater: Place a container, such as a large leaf or a piece of bark, in an open area to collect rainwater for drinking.
- Build a shelter: Use natural materials such as branches, leaves, and moss to create a structure that will protect you from wind and rain. Cover the ground with soft materials such as grass or moss to insulate yourself from the cold ground.
- Stay warm: Build a fire, wear multiple layers of clothing, and stay active to generate body heat.
- How to start a fire: Use friction, such as rubbing two sticks together, or the lens from a pair of glasses, to create a spark and start a fire for warmth and to signal for help.
- Find food: Look for edible plants, berries, or insects, and try fishing in streams or rivers if possible.
- Edible plants: Look for plants with leaves that are soft and pliable, and avoid plants with leaves that are tough or have a glossy appearance. Also, look for plants with berries or nuts that are similar to those that you recognize as edible.
- Dangerous plants: Avoid plants with leaves that are spiky or have a milky sap, as well as plants with berries or nuts that are similar to those that you recognize as poisonous. Additionally, be cautious of mushrooms and avoid eating any that have a bitter taste or that discolor when cut.
- Find North: Look for the position of the sun during the day and the stars at night to determine which direction is North.
- Build signals: Create large, visible signals such as smoke during the day and fire at night to attract attention and signal for help.
- Protect yourself from animals: Make noise and use large sticks or rocks to deter animals that may be dangerous.

- Dangerous animals: Be aware of the behavior and habitats of dangerous animals, such as snakes, bears, and large cats, and make noise to deter them if they are near. Additionally, be cautious of animals that are acting abnormally or are unafraid of humans, as these may be sick and more likely to attack.
- Conserve energy: Prioritize essential tasks and rest when possible to conserve energy and maintain physical and mental stamina.

EXTREME SURVIVAL STORIES

- In 1972, Poon Lim survived for 133 days at sea after his ship was sunk by a German submarine during World War II. He survived by catching fish and birds, and was eventually rescued by a passing ship.
- In 1972, American singer-songwriter Jim Stafford was lost in the wilderness for five days after his plane crashed in the Rocky Mountains. He survived by building a fire and eating insects, and was eventually rescued by search and rescue teams.
- In 1983, Alvaro Mangino was lost at sea for 49 days after his boat capsized in the Atlantic Ocean. He survived by drinking rainwater and eating raw fish, and was eventually rescued by a passing ship.
- In 2015, Juliane Koepcke survived a plane crash in the Amazon rainforest. She was the only survivor of the crash and spent 10 days in the jungle, surviving on bananas and drinking rainwater before being rescued by loggers.
- In 1985, a Uruguayan rugby team survived for 72 days in the Andes Mountains after their plane crashed. They survived by eating the flesh of their deceased companions and melting snow for drinking water.
- In 2009, Louis Zamperini, a former Olympic runner and World War II veteran, survived for 47 days at sea after his plane crashed in the Pacific Ocean. He survived by catching fish and birds, and was eventually rescued by the Japanese.

- In 1999, Eric Robbins survived for 13 days in the wilderness after his plane crashed in the Sierra Nevada Mountains. He survived by eating insects, berries, and drinking melted snow, and was eventually rescued by a search and rescue team.
- In 1820, the whaling ship Essex was attacked by a sperm whale and sank in the Pacific Ocean. The survivors, including Owen Chase and Thomas Nickerson, were adrift at sea for over 90 days and survived by eating the flesh of their deceased companions.
- In 1835, the shipwrecked sailors of the whale ship Jane were marooned on an uninhabited island in the Pacific Ocean for four years. They survived by fishing, hunting and gathering food, and by building shelter and tools.
- In 1965, Jerry "Nessmuk" Green survived for over 100 days in the wilderness of northern Canada, where he lived off the land and fished for his food.
- In 1802, the crew of the ship Liverpool Packet were adrift in the Atlantic Ocean for 101 days after their ship was damaged in a storm. They survived by catching fish and collecting rainwater, and were eventually rescued by a passing ship.

THE REAL COSTS OF FOOD

- The production of one egg requires approximately 53 gallons of water and emits an amount of greenhouse gasses equivalent to driving a car 4 miles.
- One pound of sugar requires approximately the same amount of energy as riding a bike for 10 miles to produce. The process also requires significant amounts of water and often involves the use of harmful chemicals, such as sulfur dioxide.
- One pound of corn requires approximately the same amount of energy as driving a car 18 miles to produce, and is also heavily reliant on the use of pesticides and fertilizers.
- One gallon of milk requires approximately the same amount of energy as riding a bike for 12 miles to produce, and the production of dairy products is also associated with significant methane emissions.
- One pound of palm oil requires approximately the same amount of energy as driving a car 160 miles to produce and is often associated with deforestation and habitat destruction.
- One pound of beef requires approximately the same amount of energy as driving a car 60 miles to produce, and the production of meat is also associated with significant greenhouse gas emissions and deforestation.
- One pound of coffee requires approximately the same amount of energy as riding a bike for 2 miles to produce, and the process is often associated with the use of harmful chemicals, such as pesticides.

- One pound of apples requires approximately the same amount of energy as riding a bike for 1.5 miles to produce, and the production of fruits and vegetables is often reliant on the use of pesticides and fertilizers.
- One pound of soybeans requires approximately the same amount of energy as driving a car 23 miles to produce, and is often associated with deforestation and habitat destruction.
- One pound of wheat requires approximately the same amount of energy as driving a car 20 miles to produce, and is also heavily reliant on the use of pesticides and fertilizers.
- The world's largest producer of almonds is not California, as many people believe, but actually Spain.
- The average chicken in the United States is given only about 72 square inches of living space, which is about the size of an iPad screen.
- Chocolate is made from the seeds of a fruit that grows on cacao trees, and the seeds must be fermented, dried, roasted, and ground to make chocolate.
- More than 70% of the world's honeybee colonies have disappeared due to a phenomenon known as Colony Collapse Disorder, which is caused by a combination of factors including pesticides, climate change, and disease.
- The process of making tofu involves boiling soybeans, grinding them into a paste, and then curdling the paste with a coagulant, similar to the process of making cheese.
- The average American eats about 60 pounds of beef per year, which requires over 1,800 gallons of water to produce.
- Nearly 50% of the fish caught globally are thrown back into the ocean as bycatch, which is a term used to describe unwanted fish that are caught accidentally while fishing for other species.
- The production of a single hamburger requires 660 gallons of water, which is equivalent to 2 months' worth of showers.
- One pound of chicken requires approximately the same amount of energy as driving a car 50 miles to produce, and the production of poultry is also associated with significant greenhouse gas emissions and the use of antibiotics.
- One pound of rice requires approximately the same amount of energy as riding a bike for 5 miles to produce, and the production of rice is often reliant on the use of pesticides and fertilizers.
- One gallon of orange juice requires approximately the same amount of energy as riding a bike for 20 miles to produce, and the production of citrus fruits is often reliant on the use of pesticides and fertilizers.
- One pound of potatoes requires approximately the same amount of energy as riding a bike for 3 miles to produce, and the production of potatoes is often reliant on the use of pesticides and fertilizers.

- One pound of carrots requires approximately the same amount of energy as riding a bike for 2 miles to produce, and the production of carrots is often reliant on the use of pesticides and fertilizers.
- One pound of avocados requires approximately the same amount of energy as driving a car 120 miles to produce, and the production of avocados is often associated with the use of pesticides and the destruction of natural habitats.
- One gallon of olive oil requires approximately the same amount of energy as riding a bike for 25 miles to produce, and the production of olives is often reliant on the use of pesticides and fertilizers.
- One pound of almonds requires approximately the same amount of energy as driving a car 160 miles to produce, and the production of almonds is often associated with the use of water-intensive irrigation and the use of pesticides.
- One pound of salmon requires approximately the same amount of energy as driving a car 90 miles to produce, and the production of fish is also associated with the use of harmful chemicals, such as pesticides, and the destruction of natural habitats.
- One pound of lettuce requires approximately the same amount of energy as riding a bike for 1 mile to produce, and the production of lettuce is often reliant on the use of pesticides and fertilizers.

IS IT FOOD? CAN I EAT IT ANYWAYS?

- The flavor of black licorice is actually derived from a plant called anise, not licorice root.
- There are more than 10,000 varieties of tomatoes, but only a few are commonly found in grocery stores.
- Nutmeg is actually the seed of a tropical fruit, and nutmeg butter, which is used in cooking, is made from the seed's flesh.
- The red color in red velvet cake is actually not from red food coloring, but from the reaction of cocoa powder with vinegar and buttermilk.
- The "five second rule" for dropped food is actually a myth, and bacteria can transfer to food immediately upon contact with a contaminated surface.
- The "apples" in Apple Jacks cereal are actually shaped like apples, but they are not made from real apples.
- The "juice" in fruit juice drinks is often not made from real fruit, but from a concentrate that is reconstituted with water and sweeteners.
- The main ingredient in Worcestershire sauce is anchovies, which give the sauce its distinct flavor.
- The hotdog is actually a type of sausage, not a distinct food item, and the term "hotdog" is used to refer to a sausage served in a bun.

- The flavor of bubblegum is actually derived from wintergreen, not from real gum.
- The "spice" in pumpkin pie spice is actually a blend of cinnamon, nutmeg, ginger, and allspice, and not a single spice.
- The white "stuff" on top of boiled eggs is actually a type of protein called albumen, and it is not mold or spoiled egg.
- The "flour" in self-raising flour is actually baking powder, and the flour is called self-raising because the baking powder allows the dough to rise without the need for yeast.
- The "cream" in whipped cream is actually heavy whipping cream, and the process of whipping the cream incorporates air, which gives the cream its light and fluffy texture.
- The "pink" in pink lemonade is actually not from real lemons, but from the addition of cranberry or raspberry juice.
- The "fruit" in fruit snacks is often not real fruit, but a mixture of sugar, corn syrup, and artificial flavors and colors.
- The "lemon" in lemon-flavored candy is actually not from real lemons, but from a combination of citric acid and artificial flavors and colors.
- The "cheddar" in cheddar cheese is actually a type of cheese, not a specific flavor or ingredient.
- The "vanilla" in vanilla extract is actually derived from the seed pods of a tropical orchid, not from a vanilla bean.
- The "red" in red candy is often not from real fruit, but from the addition of artificial colors, such as food coloring.
- The "raspberry" in raspberry jam is often not from real raspberries, but from a mixture of sugar, corn syrup, and artificial flavors and colors.
- The "apple" in apple juice is often not from real apples, but from a concentrate that is reconstituted with water and sweeteners.
- The "lemon" in lemonade is often not from real lemons, but from a mixture of lemon juice concentrate and artificial flavors and colors.
- The "orange" in orange juice is often not from real oranges, but from a concentrate that is reconstituted with water and sweeteners.
- The "grape" in grape jelly is often not from real grapes, but from a mixture of grape juice concentrate and artificial flavors and colors.
- The "strawberry" in strawberry ice cream is often not from real strawberries, but from a mixture of artificial flavors and colors.
- The "chocolate" in chocolate syrup is often not from real chocolate, but from a mixture of cocoa powder, sugar, and artificial flavors and colors.

DO MARKETERS LIE?

- "Pure honey" is often mixed with sugar, corn syrup, or other sweeteners and only contains a small amount of real honey.
- "Genuine leather" products are often made from lower quality leather scraps or synthetic materials and only have a thin layer of real leather on the surface.
- "Cashmere" products are often made from lower quality wool or synthetic materials and only have a small amount of real cashmere in the blend.
- "Pure silk" products are often made from synthetic silk or a blend of silk and other materials and only have a small amount of real silk in the product.
- "Real fur" products are often made from synthetic materials, such as acrylic or polyester, and are marketed as real fur to trick consumers.
- "Pure essential oils" are often mixed with synthetic fragrances, alcohol, or other ingredients and only contain a small amount of real essential oil.
- "Handmade" products are often made by machine or by workers in a factory and only finished by hand, rather than being made entirely by hand.
- "Organic" products are often not certified organic and may contain synthetic ingredients or be grown with the use of synthetic pesticides and fertilizers.
- "Natural" products are often not made from natural ingredients and may contain synthetic ingredients, such as artificial colors, flavors, or preservatives.
- "Antique" products are often reproductions or replicas and are marketed as genuine antiques to trick consumers.
- "Gourmet" coffee is often made from lower quality coffee beans and only contains a small amount of high-quality beans.
- "Artisanal" bread is often mass-produced in a factory and only shaped and baked by hand, rather than being made entirely by hand.

- "Herbal supplements" are often made from synthetic ingredients and only contain a small amount of real herbs.
- "Designer" clothing is often made from lower quality materials and only finished with designer labels, rather than being made entirely by the designer.
- "Premium" pet food is often made from lower quality ingredients and only contains a small amount of high-quality ingredients.
- "Hand-carved" wooden products are often made by machine and only finished by hand, rather than being made entirely by hand.
- "Vintage" products are often reproductions or replicas and are marketed as genuine vintage to trick consumers.
- "Exotic" spices are often made from lower quality ingredients and only contain a small amount of high-quality spices.
- "Luxury" skincare products are often made from lower quality ingredients and only contain a small amount of high-quality ingredients.
- "Handmade" soap is often made by machine and only cut and packaged by hand, rather than being made entirely by hand.
- "Wild-caught" seafood is often farmed or aquacultured and only contains a small amount of wild-caught seafood.
- "Artisanal" cheese is often mass-produced in a factory and only shaped and packaged by hand, rather than being made entirely by hand.
- "Organic" cosmetics are often not certified organic and may contain synthetic ingredients or be produced using synthetic processes.
- "Sustainable" wood products are often not sustainably sourced and may come from illegally logged forests or areas with poor environmental practices.
- "Artisanal" chocolate is often mass-produced in a factory and only finished by hand, rather than being made entirely by hand.
- "Craft" beers are often produced in large breweries and only have a small amount of craft beer in the blend.
- "Artisanal" pastries are often mass-produced in a factory and only finished by hand, rather than being made entirely by hand.
- "Handmade" pottery is often made by machine and only finished by hand, rather than being made entirely by hand.
- "Small batch" spirits are often mass-produced in large distilleries and only have a small amount of small-batch spirits in the blend.
- "Herbal" teas are often made from lower quality herbs and only contain a small amount of high-quality herbs.

SUPERHUMAN SENSES

- ❖ Superhuman Vision: People like Peter Bramley, also known as "Eagle Eye", have the ability to see far beyond the normal human range. Peter can spot a playing card from over a mile away and can identify individual blades of grass from a distance.
- ❖ Enhanced Hearing: People like Neil Harbisson, who was born with achromatopsia (color blindness), have the ability to hear sounds that are beyond the normal human range. Neil has a device implanted in his head that converts colors into sounds, allowing him to "hear" the world in a completely new way.
- ❖ Hyperosmia: People like Dawn Contos have the condition of hyperosmia, a heightened sense of smell. Dawn can detect scents that are undetectable to others and can identify specific fragrances from a distance.
- ❖ Supertasting: People like Tim van der Vliet have the ability to taste flavors that are beyond the normal human range. Tim can detect subtle differences in taste that others cannot and has a palate that is highly attuned to different textures and sensations.
- ❖ Prodigious Touch: People like Daniel Kish, who is blind, have the ability to feel textures and sensations that are beyond the normal human range. Daniel uses echolocation to navigate his environment and can identify objects by touch alone.
- ❖ Echolocation: People like Ben Underwood, who was born blind, have the ability to navigate their environment through sound alone. Ben uses clicks to create echoes that allow him to locate objects and obstacles in his surroundings.
- ❖ Synesthesia: People like Richard E. Cytowic have synesthesia, a condition where they experience sensory information in multiple senses. Richard can see sounds, taste colors, and hear shapes, giving him a unique perspective on the world.
- ❖ Hyperkinesia: People like Keith John, who has a rare genetic disorder called hyperkinesia, have an increased sensitivity to movement. Keith can detect even the slightest changes in his environment and is highly attuned to the movements of others.
- ❖ Temperature Sensitivity: People like Thermisol have an increased sensitivity to temperature. Thermisol can feel temperature changes that are imperceptible to others and is highly attuned to fluctuations in temperature in his environment.
- ❖ Pain Perception: People like Jo Cameron have a heightened sensitivity to pain, allowing them to feel even the slightest discomfort. Conversely, people like Tim Cridland have a reduced sensitivity to pain, allowing them to tolerate extreme pain without feeling discomfort.
- ❖ Hyperthymesia: People like Jill Price, who have the condition known as hyperthymesia, have the ability to recall nearly every day of their lives in vivid detail.

- Enhanced Smell: People like Joy Milne, who have an increased sensitivity to scent, have the ability to detect diseases like Parkinson's by their scent alone.
- Supertasting: People like Bob Holmes, who have the ability to detect flavors that are beyond the normal human range, have been used by food and beverage companies to develop new products.
- Prodigious Touch: People like J.D. Scott, who have an increased sensitivity to touch, have been used to develop new prosthetics and other assistive devices for those with disabilities.
- Hyperacusis: People like David Stock, who have the condition known as hyperacusis, have an increased sensitivity to sound, making it difficult for them to tolerate even mild sounds.
- Extreme Pain Tolerance: People like Tim Cridland, also known as "Zamora the Torture King", have a reduced sensitivity to pain, allowing them to perform stunts and acts that would be unbearable for most people.
- Hyperkinesia: People like Keith John, who have the condition known as hyperkinesia, have an increased sensitivity to movement, allowing them to perform feats of agility and coordination that are beyond the normal human range.
- Hyperthermia: People like Wim Hof, who have the ability to control their body temperature, have been able to withstand extreme cold and heat conditions.
- Photographic Memory: People like Kim Peek, who have the ability to recall complex images and scenes in intricate detail after seeing them just once, have been used to develop memory training programs and strategies.

BAD-ASS WOMEN YOU SHOULD KNOW ABOUT

- ❖ Marie Curie: Marie Curie broke down barriers for women in science at a time when it was largely a male-dominated field. She made pioneering contributions to the fields of physics and chemistry, including the discovery of two new elements, and was the first woman to win a Nobel Prize.
- ❖ Malala Yousafzai: Despite the Taliban's ban on girls' education and the threat of violence against her and her family, Malala continued to speak out for the right of girls to receive an education. She was eventually shot by a Taliban gunman but survived and continued her activism, becoming a global advocate for girls' education.
- ❖ Ruth Bader Ginsburg: In a time when women faced significant barriers in the legal profession, Ruth Bader Ginsburg challenged gender discrimination in a series of landmark cases before the Supreme Court and became a champion for women's rights.
- ❖ Frida Kahlo: Frida Kahlo faced numerous physical and emotional challenges in her life, including a near-fatal bus accident and a lifetime of chronic pain. Despite these difficulties, she used her art to express her pain and her feminist views, and became a symbol of resilience and strength.
- ❖ Harriet Tubman: Harriet Tubman escaped from slavery and risked her own safety to help hundreds of other enslaved people escape to freedom through the Underground Railroad. Despite the dangers she faced, she never stopped fighting for the abolition of slavery and for the rights of black people.
- ❖ Maya Angelou: Maya Angelou overcame a childhood filled with poverty, abuse, and racism to become a powerful voice for marginalized communities through her writing. She used her own experiences to shed light on the challenges faced by black women and to advocate for social and racial justice.
- ❖ Amelia Earhart: Amelia Earhart faced numerous challenges as a female aviator in a male-dominated field, including being told she was too small and too weak to fly. Despite these obstacles, she went on to make history as the first woman to fly solo across the Atlantic Ocean and to inspire generations of women to pursue careers in aviation.
- ❖ Sandra Day O'Connor: Sandra Day O'Connor became the first woman to serve as a US Supreme Court justice at a time when women faced significant barriers in the legal profession. She used her position to break down those barriers and to make significant contributions to American jurisprudence.
- ❖ Wangari Maathai: Wangari Maathai founded the Green Belt Movement in Kenya, which has helped to plant tens of millions of trees and to address environmental degradation and poverty. She faced numerous challenges, including government repression, in her activism but remained a powerful voice for environmental and political activism.
- ❖ Hillary Rodham Clinton: Hillary Rodham Clinton has faced numerous challenges in her political career, including being the first woman to run for president as the nominee of a major political party in the United States. Despite these obstacles, she has remained a powerful advocate for women's rights, gender equality, and

human rights, and continues to be a role model for women and girls around the world.

- Aung San Suu Kyi: Aung San Suu Kyi is a Burmese politician and Nobel laureate who has spent much of her life advocating for democracy and human rights in Myanmar. Despite being placed under house arrest for many years, she continued to work for change and eventually became the country's state counsellor.
- Irena Sendler: Irena Sendler was a Polish nurse who saved the lives of thousands of Jewish children during the Holocaust by smuggling them out of the Warsaw Ghetto. Despite being caught and tortured by the Gestapo, she never gave up the names of the children or the families who sheltered them.
- Jane Goodall: Jane Goodall is a British primatologist who has dedicated her life to the study of chimpanzees and the protection of their habitats. She has faced numerous challenges, including being denied access to her research subjects and facing skepticism from the scientific community, but has persevered to become a world-renowned expert in her field.
- Nadia Murad: Nadia Murad is a Yazidi human rights activist who survived sexual slavery at the hands of ISIS in Iraq and now advocates for the rights of survivors of sexual violence and human trafficking. Despite facing threats and opposition, she continues to speak out and to raise awareness of these issues.
- Valentina Tereshkova: Valentina Tereshkova was the first woman to fly in space and a pioneering figure in the Soviet space program. Despite facing significant obstacles as a woman in a male-dominated field, she went on to make history and to inspire generations of women to pursue careers in science and engineering.
- Wang Wei: Wang Wei was a Chinese poet and painter of the Tang dynasty who broke with convention by writing poems in a simple, colloquial style. Despite facing criticism from the literary establishment, she became one of the most celebrated poets of her time and continues to be widely read and admired.
- Wang Zhenyi: Wang Zhenyi was a Chinese astronomer, mathematician, and poet who made important contributions to the study of eclipses and the tides. Despite facing significant obstacles as a woman in a male-dominated field, she went on to become one of China's most celebrated scientists and continues to inspire women in science.
- Wilma Rudolph: Wilma Rudolph was an American sprinter who overcame childhood illness and physical disabilities to become the first American woman to win three gold medals in track and field in a single Olympics. She broke down barriers for women in sport and remains an inspiration to athletes around the world.
- Yaa Asantewaa: Yaa Asantewaa was a Ghanaian queen mother who led a successful military campaign against British colonial rule in 1900. Despite facing significant opposition, she rallied her people and led them to victory, becoming

one of Africa's most celebrated leaders and a symbol of resistance against colonialism.

- ❖ Zaha Hadid: Zaha Hadid was an Iraqi-British architect who broke down barriers for women in a male-dominated field and became one of the world's most celebrated architects. Despite facing significant challenges, including discrimination and opposition from the architectural establishment, she went on to design some of the world's most iconic buildings and to inspire generations of women in architecture.
- ❖ Boudicca: Boudicca was a queen of the Iceni tribe in ancient Britain who led a rebellion against Roman rule in the 1st century AD. Despite facing a vastly superior military force, she inspired her people to rise up and to resist the invaders, earning her a place in history as one of Britain's most celebrated leaders.
- ❖ Hatshepsut: Hatshepsut was a female pharaoh of ancient Egypt who ruled for over 20 years and oversaw a period of prosperity and expansion. Despite facing opposition from some quarters, she demonstrated her political savvy and her military prowess, becoming one of the most successful rulers in Egyptian history.
- ❖ Artemisia I of Caria: Artemisia I of Caria was a queen of ancient Caria who fought alongside the Persians against the Greeks in the Battle of Artemisium. Despite facing significant opposition, she demonstrated her courage and her military skill, earning her a place in history as one of the ancient world's most celebrated female leaders.
- ❖ Cleopatra: Cleopatra was the last ruler of ancient Egypt and one of the most famous women in history. Despite facing significant challenges, including political instability and military conflict, she demonstrated her political savvy and her charisma, becoming one of the ancient world's most powerful rulers.
- ❖ Elisabeth Báthory: Elisabeth Báthory was a countess in Hungary who earned a place in history as one of the world's most notorious serial killers. Despite facing numerous challenges, including political opposition and social stigma, she went on to become one of the most feared figures of her time.
- ❖ Joan of Arc: Joan of Arc was a French peasant girl who led her country's army to victory against the English in the Hundred Years' War. Despite facing significant opposition, including charges of heresy, she demonstrated her military skill and her unwavering determination, becoming one of the most celebrated figures in French history.
- ❖ Lady Murasaki: Lady Murasaki was a Japanese noblewoman who wrote the world's first novel, "The Tale of Genji". Despite facing significant challenges, including social and political opposition, she went on to become one of the most celebrated writers of her time and a pioneering figure in the world of literature.
- ❖ Nefertiti: Nefertiti was the wife of the Pharaoh Akhenaten and one of ancient Egypt's most famous queens. Despite facing significant challenges, including political opposition and religious controversy, she demonstrated her political

savvy and her cultural influence, becoming one of the most powerful women in ancient Egyptian history.

- Queen Mother Idia: Queen Mother Idia was a powerful queen mother of the Kingdom of Benin in what is now Nigeria. Despite facing significant opposition, she demonstrated her political savvy and her military prowess, becoming one of the most influential figures in the history of the Kingdom of Benin.
- Theodora: Theodora was a Byzantine empress who rose from humble beginnings to become one of the most powerful women in the Byzantine Empire. Despite facing significant challenges, including political opposition and religious controversy, she demonstrated her political savvy and her cultural influence, becoming one of the most celebrated figures in Byzantine history.

MEEEOOOWWW

- Some cats have a habit of watching TV, and will become fascinated by moving images and sounds, especially those of birds and other small prey.
- Cats can make over 100 different sounds, while dogs can only make about 10.
- Cats are able to drink saltwater, which can help them stay hydrated if they are lost at sea or in a desert.
- Cats can move their ears 180 degrees, allowing them to hear sounds from all directions.
- Cats are able to rotate their ears independently, allowing them to focus on multiple sounds at once.
- Cats have a flexible spine and can rotate their bodies up to 90 degrees, which helps them to fit into tight spaces and escape danger.

- Cats have a unique collar bone structure that allows them to always land on their feet, even if they fall from a great height.
- Cats can run at speeds up to 30 miles per hour, making them one of the fastest animals of their size.
- Cats have a third eyelid, also known as a nictitating membrane, which can protect their eyes and keep them moist.
- Cats have a gland in their cheeks that produces pheromones, which they use to mark their territory and communicate with other cats.
- Cats have a remarkable sense of balance and are able to perform acrobatics and stunts that are impressive even for animals much larger than them.
- Some cats have a habit of eating inedible objects, such as plastic bags, paper, and rubber bands, which is known as pica and can be harmful to their health.
- Some cats have a habit of drinking from running water, such as a tap or faucet, and will refuse to drink still water.
- Some cats have a habit of exhibiting phantom pregnancies, where they will show all the signs of being pregnant, including lactation and nest-building, even though they are not actually carrying kittens.
- Some cats have a habit of twitching their tails when they are hunting, which is thought to be a way of attracting their prey's attention.
- Some cats have a habit of kneading with their paws and purring loudly when they are happy or content, which is a sign of affection and comfort.
- Some cats have a habit of stealing and hiding objects, such as toys, coins, and even socks, which is thought to be a form of play or hoarding behavior.
- Some cats have a habit of "chirping" or "trilling" when they are happy or excited, which is a unique form of vocal communication not found in other animals.
- Some cats have a habit of playing with their food before eating it, which is thought to be a remnant of their hunting behavior.
- Some cats have a habit of appearing to be "smiling" when they are relaxed and content, with their lips pulled back to reveal their teeth in a relaxed, almost grin-like expression.

WOOF!

- Some dogs have the ability to detect certain medical conditions, such as low blood sugar levels in people with diabetes, and can alert their owners to seek medical attention.
- Some dogs have the ability to predict natural disasters, such as earthquakes and tsunamis, by detecting subtle changes in the environment and behavior of animals.
- Certain breeds of dogs, such as the Basenji and the Shiba Inu, are capable of making a wide range of vocalizations that are unique to their breed, and are not found in other dog breeds.
- Some dogs have a remarkable ability to navigate, and are capable of finding their way home over long distances, even when lost or separated from their owners.
- Certain breeds of dogs, such as the Border Collie and the Australian Cattle Dog, have an incredible ability to learn and perform complex tasks, and are capable of working with humans to achieve specific goals.
- Some dogs have the ability to communicate with humans through eye contact, body language, and vocal cues, and are capable of forming deep and complex emotional bonds with their owners.
- Some dogs have a remarkable ability to detect and respond to changes in the environment, such as changes in temperature, light levels, and air quality, and can alert their owners to potential dangers.
- Certain breeds of dogs, such as the Bloodhound and the Basset Hound, have an incredible sense of smell, and are capable of tracking scents over long distances and detecting scents that are beyond the range of human perception.

- Some dogs have a remarkable ability to learn and use human technology, such as smartphones, tablet computers, and home automation systems, and are capable of using these tools to interact with their owners.
- Some dogs have a unique ability to form close and lasting bonds with other animals, such as horses, cats, and birds, and are capable of forming complex social relationships with these animals.
- Some dogs have the ability to dream, and their sleep patterns and movements are similar to those of humans.
- Certain breeds of dogs, such as the Whippet and the Greyhound, have an incredible ability to run, and are capable of reaching speeds of up to 45 miles per hour.
- Some dogs have a remarkable ability to sense and respond to human emotions, and are capable of providing comfort and support to people who are experiencing stress, anxiety, or depression.
- Certain breeds of dogs, such as the Belgian Malinois and the German Shepherd, have a highly developed sense of protection, and are capable of working as guard dogs, police dogs, and military dogs.
- Some dogs have the ability to understand and respond to human speech, and are capable of following complex commands and directions given by their owners.
- Certain breeds of dogs, such as the Newfoundland and the Saint Bernard, have a remarkable ability to swim, and are capable of rescuing people from drowning.
- Some dogs have a remarkable ability to learn and perform tricks, and are capable of performing a wide range of acrobatic and athletic feats.
- Certain breeds of dogs, such as the Jack Russell Terrier and the Australian Terrier, have a highly developed sense of play, and are capable of playing games and having fun for hours on end.
- Some dogs have a remarkable ability to navigate, and are capable of finding their way home over long distances, even when lost or separated from their owners.
- Certain breeds of dogs, such as the Dachshund and the Basset Hound, have a highly developed sense of smell, and are capable of detecting scents that are beyond the range of human perception, and are used as hunting dogs.
- Some dogs have the ability to see ultraviolet light, and can detect things that are invisible to the human eye.
- Certain breeds of dogs, such as the Chinese Crested and the Mexican Hairless, are hairless, and have a unique set of physical adaptations that allow them to regulate their body temperature in extreme temperatures.
- Some dogs have a remarkable ability to sense and respond to changes in the Earth's magnetic field, and can use this ability to navigate and find their way home.

- Certain breeds of dogs, such as the Afghan Hound and the Saluki, have an incredibly long and slender physique, and are capable of reaching speeds of up to 65 miles per hour.
- Some dogs have a remarkable ability to survive in extreme environments, such as the Arctic, and are capable of surviving on limited food and water supplies for extended periods of time.
- Certain breeds of dogs, such as the Chihuahua and the Pomeranian, are incredibly small, and are capable of fitting into spaces that are too small for most other dogs.
- Some dogs have a remarkable ability to sense and respond to changes in atmospheric pressure, and can use this ability to predict weather changes and natural disasters.
- Certain breeds of dogs, such as the Basenji and the Shiba Inu, have a unique vocalization, and are capable of making a wide range of sounds that are not found in other dog breeds.
- Some dogs have a remarkable ability to sense and respond to changes in the environment, and can use this ability to detect and avoid danger.
- Certain breeds of dogs, such as the Bichon Frise and the Poodle, have a highly developed sense of intuition, and are capable of detecting and responding to human emotions and thoughts.

INCREDIBLE ANIMAL ADAPTATIONS

- The long-tailed macaque, a type of monkey found in Southeast Asia, has learned to use tools such as rocks and sticks to crack open hard-shelled nuts and fruit. This is an example of the monkey's advanced problem-solving skills and ability to learn from its environment.
- The African elephant has evolved to have an extremely long and flexible trunk, which they use for grasping food, drinking water, and communicating with other elephants. The trunks are actually a fusion of the elephant's upper lip and nose, and contain over 100,000 muscles.
- The Arctic fox is able to survive in extremely cold temperatures by growing a thick, white coat of fur during the winter months, which provides insulation and camouflage. In the summer, the fox's coat turns brown to blend in with its surroundings.
- The kangaroo rat, found in the deserts of North America, is able to live without drinking water by obtaining moisture from the seeds and plants it eats. The rat has also evolved to conserve water by producing dry feces and urine.
- The vampire bat has evolved to have razor-sharp teeth and a special enzyme in its saliva that allows it to feed on the blood of other animals. The bat's saliva

contains an anticoagulant that prevents the blood from clotting, making it easier for the bat to feed.

- ❖ The bombardier beetle has the ability to spray hot, noxious chemicals from its body as a form of self-defense against predators. The beetle can aim its spray with precision and can produce a series of rapid-fire blasts.
- ❖ The cuttlefish is able to change the texture and color of its skin to blend in with its surroundings and communicate with other cuttlefish. This is accomplished through special skin cells called chromatophores, which can be expanded or contracted to create different patterns and colors.
- ❖ The octopus has the ability to camouflage itself by changing the color and texture of its skin to blend in with its surroundings. The octopus can also release ink to distract predators and make its escape.
- ❖ The fennec fox, found in the deserts of North Africa, has large ears that help it to regulate its body temperature and hear prey moving in the sand. The fox's ears also have fur on the inside to help protect against the hot desert sun.
- ❖ The sand gazelle, found in the deserts of the Middle East, has evolved to have large, flat hooves that allow it to run quickly over loose sand without sinking. The gazelle's hooves are also padded with special shock-absorbing tissues to protect against impact.
- ❖ The green sea turtle has the ability to navigate long distances using Earth's magnetic field, which helps it to find its way back to its nesting site. The turtle's brain contains a small amount of magnetite, which allows it to sense the Earth's magnetic field.
- ❖ The naked mole-rat, found in the deserts of East Africa, is able to live in underground tunnels with very little oxygen by regulating its body temperature and breathing rate. The rat's skin is also specially adapted to allow it to absorb oxygen directly from the ai
- ❖ The archerfish, found in the rivers and estuaries of Southeast Asia, is able to shoot jets of water at insects and other prey, knocking them into the water where they can be easily eaten. The fish has the ability to accurately aim its shot by adjusting the position of its mouth and tongue.
- ❖ The mountain goat, found in the high elevations of North America, has evolved to have hooves with rubbery pads that allow it to grip and climb steep, rocky terrain. The goat is also able to jump up to six feet in a single leap.
- ❖ The bowerbird, found in the rainforests of Australia, is able to build elaborate, decorated nests to attract a mate. The bird uses sticks, leaves, and other materials to create an artistic display that showcases its creativity and resourcefulness.
- ❖ The Nile crocodile has evolved to have extremely strong jaws and sharp teeth, which it uses to catch and devour large prey such as antelope and wildebeest. The crocodile's jaw muscles can generate over 1,000 pounds of force per square inch.

- The sloth has evolved to have long, curved claws that allow it to grip tree branches and hang upside down without falling. The sloth's metabolism is also adapted to slow down significantly, allowing it to conserve energy and move slowly.
- The proboscis monkey, found in the rainforests of Southeast Asia, has a large, bulbous nose that helps it to attract a mate and communicate with other monkeys. The monkey's nose is also thought to play a role in regulating its body temperature.
- The snowshoe hare, found in the forests of North America, has evolved to have white fur during the winter months, which provides camouflage against the snow. In the summer, the hare's fur turns brown to blend in with the forest floor.
- The frilled lizard, found in the forests of Australia and New Guinea, has evolved to have a large, frill-like collar around its neck that it can expand when threatened. The lizard's frill is actually made up of skin and cartilage, and is used to intimidate predators.
- The giant anteater, found in the forests of South America, has evolved to have a long, sticky tongue that it uses to capture ants and termites. The anteater's tongue can be up to two feet long and is covered in tiny, backward-facing spines.
- The anglerfish, found in the deep waters of the ocean, has evolved to have a glowing lure on the end of a long filament that it uses to attract prey. The fish's mouth is also lined with sharp teeth, allowing it to devour prey that is much larger than itself.
- The giraffe has evolved to have a long, flexible neck that allows it to reach high branches for food. The giraffe's neck contains just seven vertebrae, but each one can be up to 10 inches long.

MYSTERIOUS DISAPPEARANCES OF FAMOUS PEOPLE

- ❖ The vanishing of Elisabeth d'Agoult in 1848 remains one of the most mysterious disappearances of the 19th century. She disappeared without a trace, leaving behind a note saying that she was going to seek a new life. Some speculate that she may have been murdered, while others believe she may have fled to start a new life under a different identity.

- ❖ Wilbur Wright, one of the famous Wright brothers, disappeared during a flight over the English Channel in 1912. Despite extensive searches, no one has ever been able to determine what happened to him. Some speculate that his plane may have crashed into the Channel, while others believe he may have survived and started a new life under a different name.

- ❖ Gloria Morgan Vanderbilt disappeared in 1965 and her fate remains unknown. Despite extensive searches and numerous leads, no one has ever been able to determine what happened to her. Some speculate that she may have been murdered, while others believe she may have fled to start a new life.

- ❖ Percy Fawcett, the British explorer, disappeared in the Amazon in 1925 while searching for a lost city. Despite numerous expeditions and searches, no one has ever been able to determine what happened to him. Some speculate that he may have been killed by indigenous tribes, while others believe he may have found the lost city and decided to remain there.

- ❖ Thomas Parker, the American businessman, disappeared in 1917 without a trace, leaving behind a wife and children. His fate remains unknown. Some speculate that he may have been murdered, while others believe he may have fled to start a new life under a different name.

- Charles Ashmore, the American journalist, disappeared in 1918 while covering the Russian Revolution. Despite extensive searches, no one has ever been able to determine what happened to him. Some speculate that he may have been executed by the Bolsheviks, while others believe he may have fled the country to escape persecution.
- Lord Kitchener, the British aristocrat, disappeared in 1916 during a naval voyage to Russia. Despite extensive searches, no one has ever been able to determine what happened to him. Some speculate that his ship may have been sunk by a German submarine, while others believe he may have survived and started a new life under a different name.
- Paul Éluard, the French poet, disappeared in 1952 during a trip to the Soviet Union. Despite extensive searches, no one has ever been able to determine what happened to him. Some speculate that he may have been executed by the Soviets, while others believe he may have fled the country to escape persecution.
- Lowell Thomas, the American journalist, disappeared in 1950 during a trip to the Middle East. Despite extensive searches, no one has ever been able to determine what happened to him. Some speculate that he may have been kidnapped or murdered, while others believe he may have decided to start a new life in the region.
- Steve Fossett, the American aviator, disappeared in 2007 during a flight over the Nevada desert. Despite extensive searches, no one has ever been able to determine what happened to him. Some speculate that his plane may have crashed, while others believe he may have faked his own death to start a new life.
- The disappearance of Amelia Earhart in 1937 remains one of the most famous unsolved mysteries of all time. The pioneering aviator and her plane vanished without a trace during an attempted flight around the world. Some speculate that her plane may have crashed into the Pacific Ocean, while others believe she may have survived and started a new life on a remote island.
- The vanished French writer Antoine de Saint-Exupéry disappeared during a reconnaissance mission in World War II. His fate was unknown for decades until a fisherman found his silver bracelet. Some speculate that his plane was shot down by the Germans, while others believe he may have crash-landed and survived for a time before succumbing to his injuries.
- The disappearance of Jim Thompson, the American businessman and architect who became known as the "Thai silk king," remains a mystery to this day. He vanished without a trace in 1967 while on a hike in the Cameron Highlands of Malaysia. Some speculate that he may have been murdered, while others believe he may have fallen into a river and drowned.
- The mysterious disappearance of Lord Lucan in 1974 is one of the most famous cases of a missing British peer. Despite extensive searches and numerous alleged sightings, no one has been able to determine what happened to him. Some

speculate that he may have fled the country and started a new life under a different name, while others believe he may have committed suicide.

- ❖ The sudden disappearance of Glenn Miller, the popular American bandleader and trombonist, during a flight over the English Channel in 1944 has never been fully explained. Some speculate that his plane was shot down by a German aircraft, while others believe he may have survived and started a new life under a different name.

- ❖ The vanishing of the crew of the Mary Celeste in 1872 is one of the most famous maritime mysteries of all time. The ship was found adrift in the Atlantic Ocean with no one on board and no signs of foul play. Some speculate that the crew may have been lost at sea due to adverse weather conditions or an accident, while others believe they may have been murdered by pirates.

- ❖ The disappearance of Agatha Christie, the famous British crime writer, in 1926 sparked an extensive search and widespread speculation about what had happened to her. She was found 11 days later, staying at a hotel under an assumed name. Some speculate that she may have suffered from amnesia or a nervous breakdown, while others believe she may have staged her own disappearance to escape her unhappy marriage.

- ❖ The vanished American businessman Harvey Lyon was last seen in 1921, boarding a train in New York City. Despite extensive searches, no one has ever been able to determine what happened to him. Some speculate that he may have been murdered, while others believe he may have fled to start a new life under a different name.

- ❖ The disappearance of Jimmy Hoffa, the former president of the International Brotherhood of Teamsters, remains one of the most famous and enduring mysteries of modern American history. Despite numerous investigations and a number of leads, his fate remains unknown. Some speculate that he may have been murdered by organized crime figures, while others believe he may have gone into hiding to escape prosecution.

THE END... OR IS IT?

Hey, fellow trivia addicts... Did you get your fix with "Brain-Boosting Facts for Curious Minds?" Of course, you did! But don't keep that awesomeness to yourself — let the world know by leaving a review on Amazon!

As a thank you, we've got a special gift waiting for you, absolutely free! So, what are you waiting for? Sign up now and claim your brain-boosting bonus pack! Just go to:

www.hhfpress.com/brain

But that's not all, folks! We've got a whole library of mind-blowing trivia books to satisfy your curiosity cravings! From "Weird and Wonderful World Facts" to "Mind-Blowing Science Trivia," we've got it all!

So, come on down and join the trivia party! Leave us a review, grab your free gift, and dive into our other fantastic books today!

Thanks for reading!
- Daniel Kane